Philosophy of Religion

Study guide

Andrew Capone

Contents

Purpose of the Book

The OCR 2016 specification H573 has posed some challenges for teacher and student, and for this reason this guide represents the foundation of a new approach to study which integrates elements of the Peped project.

- The textbooks have produced their own interpretation of the specification, in the sense of additional authors and ideas, which you don't necessarily need to adopt or follow. They have overlaid an additional discussion of philosophers and philosophical ideas in order to evaluate the fairly brief content of the specification. So it is essential you understand that you will be examined on knowledge and content alone - and you can use whoever you like to evaluate and criticise this content.

You should download and print out now a hard copy of the relevant pages of the specification.

- The three papers need to be integrated to produce what is called synoptic insight. Here we call them Thought Points. This literally means elements of the three papers that can be 'seen together' or linked up. For example, Kant's moral argument (Philosophy of Religion) links and to his ethics which links to Jon Hick's universal pluralism (Christian Thought H573/3) as Hick is greatly inspired by Kant. The Peped website shows additional ways to integrate the three papers and there will be a revision section accessible for those who have this guide showing you how to increase your synoptic understanding.

Those who have this integrated workbook should have a head-start, but you need to supplement it with other ideas and sample answers.

- Our approach is to teach for structures of thought. These are given by the mind-maps in this workbook. Notice these are not prescriptive - you can make up your own if you wish, or amend these. But to write effective philosophical essays, you need to write according to structures of thought and not some formula for essay-writing (which you may find online). These structures are the same you will find on the peped website and in our revision guides.

- Our aim here is to help you ask the right questions, in the right order, to help you teach yourself. The workbook does not provide all the answers. This is because we want you to do our own research (using the peped site or the wider internet resources, such as the Excellent Internet Encyclopaedia of Philosophy). We will also mark your essays for you if you buy an essay-marking credit, or provide an on-line tutor for you who will provide Skype or phone support and guidance.

Philosophical Language and Thought

Ancient influences

Structure of Thought

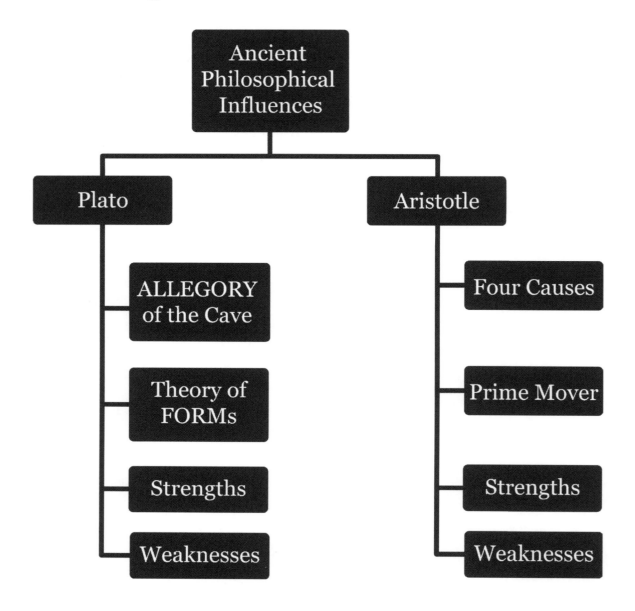

Plato

A. Allegory of the Cave

What is Knowledge?

In Republic, Plato explores the nature of knowledge and how only reason (**episteme**) can lead to true knowledge (**doxa**) as experience will only give us changing opinion.

Exercise: Define these terms: Episteme and Doxa.

The Allegory

Plato's allegory of the cave appears in The Republic. Each aspect of the allegory represents something in the real world.

Exercise: Draw a table and explain each of the symbols of the cave: The cave wall, the prisoners, the shadows, the puppets, the free prisoner, the jagged path, the sun.

The Free Prisoner

In the Allegory of the Cave Plato identifies the free prisoner as the philosopher.

Men would say of him that up he went and down he came without his eyes; and that it was better not even to think of ascending; and if any one tried to loose another and lead him up to the light, let them only catch the offender, and they would put him to death.

Exercise: What does the journey up the jagged path represent?

Why is it significant that the free prisoner does not recognise what he sees when he leaves the cave?

B. The Theory of FORMS

FORMs and Particulars

In Republic, Plato gives the example of the idea of a bed and an example of a bed.

And what of the maker of the bed? Were you not saying that he too makes, not the idea which, according to our view, is the essence of the bed, but only a particular bed?

Exercise: Explain the relationship between ideas and particulars.

Why does the example of the idea of bed (and other things that are physically instantiated) cause problems for the theory of FORMs compared with the idea of justice?

The Fool and the Philosopher

FORMs are abstract and eternal notions/ideas. We recognise the FORMs in the temporal examples we encounter in this world. The FORMs are the essence of the thing we are encountering. The Essential FORM of Goodness gives life to all other FORMs. For example, the fool sees many different trees, but the philosopher sees many examples of the true FORM of tree.

Exercise: Give examples of the essence of the following: love, beauty, vehicle.

Draw the hierarchy of FORMs; put the Essential FORM of Goodness at the top.

The Nature of the FORMs

In Cratylus, Plato discusses the nature of knowledge and how we can distinguish between examples and true knowledge. The essence is apart from the many examples.

For neither does every smith, although he may be making the same instrument for the same purpose, make them all of the same iron. The form must be the same, but the material may vary, and still the instrument may be equally good of whatever iron made, whether in Hellas or in a foreign country; there is no difference.

Later, Plato argued that knowledge of things changes over time, so no true knowledge can be gained from physical examples of things.

But if the very nature of knowledge changes, at the time when the change occurs there will be no knowledge, and, according to this view, there will be no one to know and nothing to be known: but if that which knows and that which is known exist ever, and the beautiful and the good and every other thing also exist, then I do not think that they can resemble a process of flux, as we were just now supposing.

Exercise: How does Plato distinguish between the FORM of an object and a material example?

Explain how Plato argues that things can be known if everything we encounter is in constant flux.

C. Evaluating Plato

Influences on Plato

Plato's theory was built on many ideas that circulated around his time, primarily from Parmenides' notion of the fixed world, Heraclitus' notion of the world in flux, Pythagoras' abstract mathematics and Socrates' notion of knowledge coming from reason.

Democritus was a Greek thinker. He postulated that things in the world could be divided continuously, but at some point they could not be divided anymore and we would arrive at non-divisibles, or a-toms. In the 20th Century scientists thought they had discovered these non-divisibles and called them atoms.

> **Exercise:** Create a mind-map explaining the influences on Plato's theory of FORMs.

Challenges to Plato's Theory

There are three main challenges to the theory of FORMs, the first two presented by Aristotle, Plato's student:

1. Every FORM is a member of a class and so needs a FORM, leading to the Third Man Fallacy.

2. If there is a FORM of everything, then there are forms of negations and poor versions of things. In Metaphysics (Book XIII Part 4) Aristotle challenges Plato's Theory of FORMs on the bases that the theory demands there to be FORMs of all sorts of unlikely things.

Of the ways in which it is proved that the Forms exist, none is convincing; for from some no inference necessarily follows, and from some arise Forms even of things of which they think there are no Forms. For according to the arguments from the sciences there will be Forms of all things of which there are sciences, and according to the argument of the 'one over many' there will be Forms even of negations, and according to the argument that thought has an object when the individual object has perished, there will be Forms of perishable things; for we have an image of these. (Republic)

In addition to this, there is a third challenge we can use: the theory of FORMs requires the belief in reincarnation which, while Pythagoras supported it, is far from certain which undermines the theory.

Exercise: Divide this page into 3 parts and summarise each of the challenges to the Theory of FORMS.

Aristotle

A. The Four Causes

Matter and Form

Aristotle gives the example of the wax stamp when discussing the distinction between matter and form. The wax is the matter and the form is the stamp imprint.

Exercise: What is the difference between Aristotelian form and Plato's notion of FORM?

Explain how one might argue that Plato's idea of essence (e.g. tree-ness) is nothing more than the labelling of a number of examples with a similar [Aristotelian] form.

Efficient and Final

Aristotle gave the example of the bronze statue when discussing the nature of the Four Causes. The efficient cause is the sculptor and the final cause is the honouring of the gods and the admiration of others. Aristotle said human being's final cause is Eudaimonia.

Exercise: What can we know about the efficient cause: from a 'tasty cake'?

Actuality and Potentiality

In Metaphysics (Book IX Part 8), Aristotle distinguished between actuality (what a thing is) and potentiality (what a thing can become). For Aristotle a thing is moved into its actuality by something prior to it. For Aristotle, the Prime Mover was pure actuality that was itself unmoved.

Obviously…the substance or form is actuality. According to this argument, then, it is obvious that actuality is prior in substantial being to potency; and as we have said, one actuality always precedes another in time right back to the actuality of the eternal prime mover.

Exercise: Draw the example of wax and a wax stamp. Label the wax's potentiality and the stamp's actuality.

B. The Prime Mover

Nature of the Prime Mover

Aristotle said that the Prime Mover causes the movement of all things, not as the efficient cause, but as the final cause of all things. This was important for two reasons: 1. an efficient cause is changed by the action of causing – and the Prime Mover is unchanging – and 2. a regression of efficient causes is infinite – as he believed there was no first efficient, just an infinite regression.

> **Exercise:** What are the similarities and differences between Plato's Essential FORM of Goodness and Aristotle's Prime Mover?

Characteristics of the Prime Mover

In Metaphysics (Book XII Part 8), Aristotle argues that the Prime Mover is perfect in goodness and simplicity.

Evidently there is but one heaven. For if there are many heavens as there are many men, the moving principles, of which each heaven will have one, will be one in form but in number many. But all things that are many in number have matter; for one and the same definition, e.g. that of man, applies to many things, while Socrates is one. But the primary essence has not matter; for it is complete reality. So the unmovable first mover is one both in definition and in number; so too, therefore, is that which is moved always and continuously; therefore there is one heaven alone.

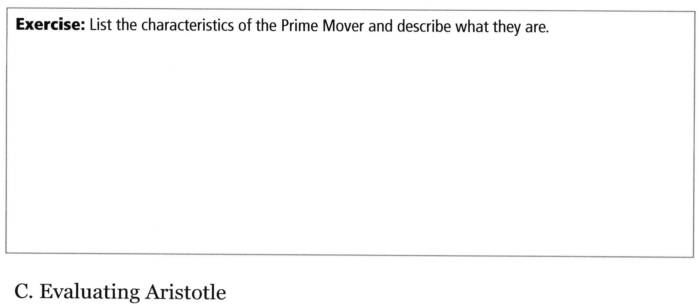

Exercise: List the characteristics of the Prime Mover and describe what they are.

C. Evaluating Aristotle

Strengths of Aristotle

The Four Causes are the basis of how human beings gain knowledge about different things. When we have a need for something, we consider the purpose, what materials we have and then we design a new device to fulfil that need. If we accidentally discover something new, we see what purpose it fulfils and then work out what it is made of and how it fulfils that purpose.

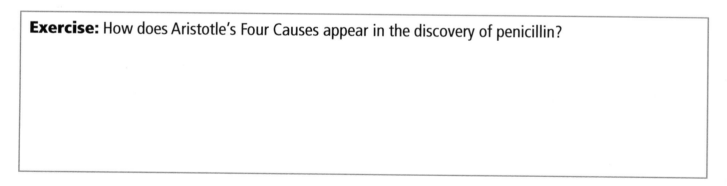

Exercise: How does Aristotle's Four Causes appear in the discovery of penicillin?

Weaknesses of Aristotle

Aristotle made a number of errors ranging from miscalculating the number of teeth in women to the number of legs on bees.

Exercise: Compare Plato's theory of FORMs to Aristotle's theory of Causes. Which is the better theory of knowledge? Defend this position with examples and evidence.

Essay Skills

Types of questions

Questions on this topic might focus on Plato's or Aristotle's theory of knowledge. Whichever it asks, candidates should always use the other in evaluation. Some examples of questions you might be asked are these:

Question	What it is asking
Episteme comes from reason, not experience.' Discuss.	You are comparing Plato's notion that knowledge comes from reason with Aristotle's notion that knowledge comes from experience.
Plato does not value experience enough.' Discuss.	Plato does not value experience, so you are evaluating whether or not he is right in this position.
Assess the claim that Aristotle's Prime Mover does not explain how things happen.	You are assessing whether the Prime Mover is a suitable theory for the nature of things as pure actuality and final cause of all things.
To what extent are Aristotle's Four Causes sufficient in explaining the world?	You are assessing the success of Aristotle's theory of Causes and then comparing it with Plato's theory of FORMs.

Exercise: Write down three relevant ideas on this question: 'Plato's theory of knowledge tells us nothing about the physical world.' Discuss.

Essay Skills – Introductions and Thesis Statement

Your introduction should:

1. indicate to the reader that you know what the question is about;

2. demonstrate the parameters of the question giving a sense of the two main sides of the argument; and

3. make clear where the essay will go, giving a clear thesis statement.

Your thesis statement is important because it shows your line of reasoning. Your essay needs to be a single rational dialogue with the reader showing that you have thought about the question and have an argument to make. You need to have an argument that you are following, otherwise you are just writing all you know about the subject. Examiners want to see that you have engaged with the question and that you know what you want to say. Even if you are unsure about the argument, you must have a thesis statement.

Avoid vague statements like: 'there are many opinions on this' or 'I will be showing the different views on this topic'. They don't tell the examiner anything. That said, if you don't agree with either position, you can form your own position: 'while Plato's notion of dualism can be defended by a modern psychological understanding of the mind, I will be showing that this psyche cannot exist disembodied'.

Exercise: Take this question: 'Aristotle's theory of Four Causes, fails to explain the nature of things.' Discuss.

Write an introduction making all three parts of the introduction clear and distinct. One sentence is enough for each, but make sure each sentence is clear and concise.

1. Position 1 – Definition and context: Identify what the question is about and present Aristotle's position.

2. Position 2 – Parameters and opposition: State the opposing position, the position of Plato.

3. Position 3 – Thesis statement: Make it clear where you stand, with Aristotle, Plato or somewhere between. Be concise, outlining what your position is.

Soul, Mind and Body

Structure of Thought

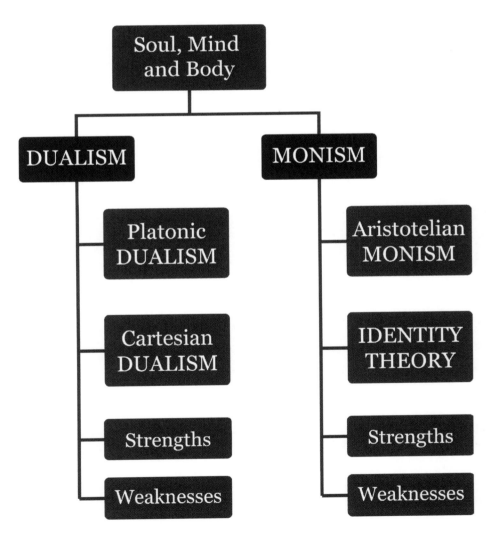

Dualism

A. Platonic Dualism

Plato was a dualist, believing that the body and soul/psyche were separate substances. In Phaedro, Plato criticises the weakness of the body.

The body is the source of endless trouble to us by reason of the mere requirement of food; and is liable also to disease which overtake and impede us in the search after true being: it fills us full of loves, and lusts, and fears, and fancies of all kinds, and endless foolery and in fact, as men say, takes away all power of thinking. (Phaedro)

Exercise: Explain the extent to which the body and the soul are distinct.

The Charioteer

As a dualist, everything Plato thought concerning knowledge rested on his belief that we pre-existed our earthly lives. Platonic dualism is demonstrated in Plato's allegory of the charioteer. By recognising the tripartite nature of the psyche, we see that the psyche is in fact separate from the body. This is NOT a proof of life after death, but of the distinct nature of the psyche compared with the body.

Exercise: Describe each of the three parts of the charioteer analogy: Charioteer, White Horse, and Black Horse.

Arguments for Life after Death

In Plato's work Cebes, Socrates is condemned to death for corrupting the youth of Athens, but refuses to take his fiends' counsel and flee the city. He argues there is nothing to fear in death. In his conversations with Cebes and Simmias in Phaedro, Socrates presents the arguments from opposites and recollection.

Men are in process of recollecting that which they learned before. …Our souls must have existed before they were in the form of man-without bodies, and must have had intelligence. …If these absolute ideas existed before we were born, then our souls must have existed before we were born, and if not the ideas, then not the souls. …The soul will exist after death as well as before birth. …Well, and is there not an opposite of life, as sleep is the opposite of waking? Then suppose you analyse Life and death to me in the same manner. Is not death opposed to life? (Cebes)

Exercise: Explain how Plato seeks to prove that life after death is possible.

Transmigration of the Soul

Plato argued that the soul transmigrates, changes from one body to another. Between lives our souls go to the world of FORMs and we encounter the FORMs. Plato illustrated this in the Myth of Er and emphasised that before our rebirth we drink from the river of forgetfulness. This is why when we experience things, we are remembering or recognising the FORMs in them which we knew in the World of FORMs.

Exercise: Summarise how you would use the Myth of Er in an essay defending disembodied existence. **Hint**: When writing an essay, keep your paragraph on Platonic dualism separate from your paragraph on Plato's arguments for life after death.

B. Cartesian Dualism

Substance Dualism

Descartes was also a proponent of dualism. He believed that the soul was a substance separate from the body and that it animated the body like the strings animated the marionette (puppet). Descartes believed that ideas and thoughts were made of a spiritual substance that existed separately from matter.

Exercise: Sort these into two lists, spiritual/ideal substance and material substances: a table, a cat, trigonometry, the colour blue, love, memories, the earth, blood.

Dual Nature of the Body and Soul

In Principles of Philosophy (Part 1, LX Of distinctions; and first of the real), Descartes discusses how we can be certain that the body and soul are two distinct substances.

Since we have now…the idea of an extended and corporeal substance…merely because we have the idea of it, we may be assured that such may exist; and, if it really exists, that every part which we can determine by thought must be really distinct from the other parts of the same substance. In the same way, since everyone is conscious that he thinks, and that he in thought can exclude from himself every other substance, whether thinking or extended, it is certain that each of us thus considered is really distinct from every other thinking and corporeal substance. (Principles of Philosophy)

Exercise: Explain Substance Dualism.

Nature of the Soul

One way of understanding Descartes' theory of the relationship between the soul and the body is by comparing it to the cardiovascular system.

System	Substance that circulates the body.	Organ that drives the substance.	Function of the substance.
Cardiovascular	Blood	Heart	Bring oxygen around the body.
Soul	Animal Spirit	Pineal Gland	Animation of the body.

Exercise: Explain the relationship between the soul and the body in Descartes theory.

Evaluating Dualism

Dr Ian Stevenson

The recent work of Dr Ian Stevenson on reincarnation adds evidence, though not conclusive proof, to the argument that people are reincarnated.

Instead of relying on hypnosis to verify that an individual has had a previous life, he instead chose to collect thousands of cases of children who spontaneously remember a past life. Dr. Ian Stevenson uses this approach because spontaneous past life memories in a child can be investigated using strict scientific protocols. In order to collect his data, Dr. Stevenson methodically documents the child's statements of a previous life. Then he identifies the deceased person the child remembers being, and verifies the facts of the deceased person's life that match the child's memory. He even matches birthmarks and birth defects to wounds and scars on the deceased, verified by medical records. His strict methods systematically rule out all possible "normal" explanations for the child's memories.

Exercise: Find some examples of Dr Ian Stevenson's research.

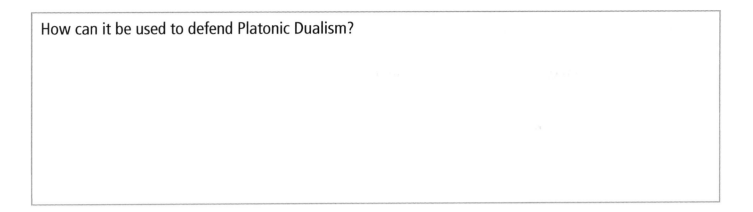

How can it be used to defend Platonic Dualism?

Anthony Kenny

Anthony Kenny defended Plato's notion that the psyche was divided into rational and non-rational. He gave the example of the toddler having a tantrum suggesting that this shows the pre-rational psyche. Some modern psychologists have argued that the body and psyche are dual in nature which is why some people feel trapped in other people's bodies.

Exercise: To what extent does modern psychology support Platonic Dualism and the belief in life after death?

Gilbert Ryle

In Concept of Mind, Gilbert Ryle challenged Descartes' dualism by calling it a category error.

It represents the facts of mental life as if they belonged to one logical type or category, when they actually belong to another. … A foreigner visiting Oxford or Cambridge for the first time is shown a number of colleges, libraries, playing fields, museums, scientific departments and administrative offices. He then asks 'But where is the University? He was mistakenly allocating the University to the same category as that to which the other institutions belong. (Concept of Mind)

Exercise: Respond to Descartes' dualistic approach using Ryle's concept of a category error.

Monism

A. Aristotelian Monism

Matter and Form

Aristotle was a monist believing that the body and soul were a hylomorphic (being - ousia - is a compound of matter and form) soul/body unity. They are inseparable. He likened this relationship to that between the wax and a stamp in De Anima (Book II Part 1).

It is as meaningless as to ask whether the wax and the shape given to it by the stamp are one, or generally the matter of a thing and that of which it is the matter. (De Anima)

Exercise: Draw a wax stamp (for making seals) and label the matter and the form.

How can the human being be compared to the wax stamp (by analogy)?

Actuality and Potentiality

In De Anima (Book II Part 1), Aristotle argued that the body was the potentiality of the person and the soul was the actuality. However, he distinguished between grades of actuality and potentiality:

The soul is the first grade of actuality of a natural body having life potentially in it. The body so described is a body which is organised. The parts of plants in spite of their extreme simplicity are 'organs'. If, then, we have to give a general formula applicable to all kinds of soul, we must describe it as the first grade of actuality of a natural organised body. That is why we can wholly dismiss as unnecessary the question whether the soul and the body are one. (De Anima)

First Potentiality (matter)	Second Potentiality/First Actuality (form)	Second Actuality (telos)
Body	Soul	Animated soul
A person with the power of speech	A person who knows how to speak French but does not	A person speaking French
Pine Wood	The puppet Pinocchio	Pinocchio animated by the Blue Fairy

Exercise: Explain the relationship between the body and the soul in Aristotle's hylomorphic soul/ body unity.

B. Identity Theory

The Mind is the Self

The position of Identity Theory is that the person is their brain, their mind and nothing more. There is no soul, nothing that is separate from the body. A person's character and personality is made from their brains.

Exercise: Explain how the position of Identity Theory contradicts the ideas of Dualism.

In what way does this also undermine the belief in life after death.

Phineas Gage

In the 1800s there was a foreman on a railway line called Phineas Gage who was well liked by his subordinates. One day he had an accident and a metal pole penetrated his head and brain. He survived but was completely different thereafter, so much so that he could no longer work as a foreman.

Exercise: Explain how the case of Phineas Gage supports the position of Identity Theory.

Richard Dawkins

Richard Dawkins is convinced that there is no spirit/soul or life after death. The only way in which anything of us survives our deaths is through our genes. Our bodies are nothing more than survival machines for the genes.

Individuals are not stable things, they are fleeting. Chromosomes too are shuffled to oblivion, like hands of cards soon after they are dealt. But the cards themselves survive the shuffling. The cards are the genes. The genes are not destroyed by crossing-over, they merely change partners and march on. Of course they march on. That is their business. They are the replicators and we are their survival machines. When we have served our purpose we are cast aside. But genes are denizens of geological time: genes are forever.

Exercise: How is Dawkins' view of the materialist relationship between genes and body similar and different to Plato's view of the dualist relationship between psyche and body?

C. Evaluating Monism

John Locke

John Locke was not an identity theorist; he did not believe that a person's identity was in the brain but in their consciousness. He gave this story to demonstrate the relationship between the body and consciousness.

There was once a Prince and a Cobbler. One day they woke up to find themselves in each other's bodies. The cobbler was anxious to explain that he had not broken into the palace, but that he had no idea how he came to be there – but because he had the appearance of the prince, no one understood what his problem was. The prince, waking up in the cobbler's body, was angry with the cobbler's wife in bed beside him, thinking she had kidnapped him, and demanded to be returned to the palace. (Locke)

Locke raised the question: which person was which? Is it the mind that makes the individual, or the body? What makes us what we are? Is it our appearance, our memories, our individual personality traits, or is it something else?

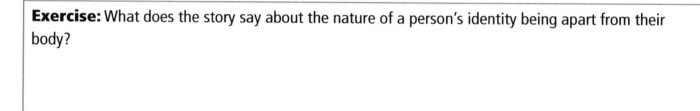

Exercise: What does the story say about the nature of a person's identity being apart from their body?

There are many movies and TV shows that explore the idea of transferring consciousness rom one person to another person or vessel. Research one example. What is a person's consciousness?

John Hick

John Hick was a monist but also believed in resurrection. He believed that when we die, God will replicate our bodies into spiritual bodies. He was adamant that dualism was not the solution. In Theology and Verification, he presented his argument.

The only self of which we know is the empirical self who lives and then dies. Mental events and mental characteristics are analysed into the modes of behaviour and behavioural dispositions of this empirical self. The human being is described as an organism capable of acting in the "high-level" ways which we characterise as intelligent, thoughtful, humorous, calculating, and the like. The concept of mind or soul is thus not the concept of a "ghost in the machine" (to use Gilbert Ryle's loaded phrase), but of the more flexible and sophisticated ways in which human beings behave and have it in them to behave. (John Hick)

Exercise: To what extent does Replica Theory resolve the problem life after death for monists?

Essay Skills

Types of questions

Questions on this topic might focus on Dualism, Monism and the question of life after death/ embodied or disembodied existence. Whichever it asks, candidates should always use the other views in evaluation. Some examples of questions you might be asked are these:

Question	What it is asking
Assess the claim that disembodied existence is impossible.	*You are evaluating the dualist position that your soul/psyche can exist separately from the body, e.g. life after death.*
It is impossible to survive one's death.' Discuss.	*You are evaluating whether there is any basis for life after death, embodied or disembodied.*
You are your brain.' Discuss.	*This is a question about Identity Theory. Start with Dawkins, the example of Phineas Gage, Ryle's attack on dualism etc. Then respond with dualist arguments. Be careful, monism is not the same as identity theory, but it should appear in this essay, perhaps as a middle-way.*
Evaluate the claim that the mind is separate from the body.	*This is a more general question distinguishing monism and dualism. Both monism and materialism support similar positions in this question, united against dualism.*

Exercise: Analyse this question: 'Embodied existence is the only form of existence.' Discuss.

Essay Skills – Defending your Thesis Statement

Your essay should read like a debate between two positions. As in a public debate, you have the house and the opposition. The house's position will be the position of the question and the opposition's will be the negation of that position, e.g. in the above question ['Embodied existence is the only form of existence.' Discuss], the house' position is: Embodied existence **is** the only form of existence; the opposition's position is: Embodied existence is **not** the only form of existence. Note, the opposition only needs to prove the House wrong.

Once you have written your introduction and thesis statement, your essay should be balanced, showing both sides of the debate. However, since your thesis statement states your position, there should be more arguments supporting your thesis statement.

Exercise: Write a thesis statement for the above question. Write three arguments defending your position and two arguments challenging it.

Arguments for God's Existence

A Priori Arguments

Structure of Thought

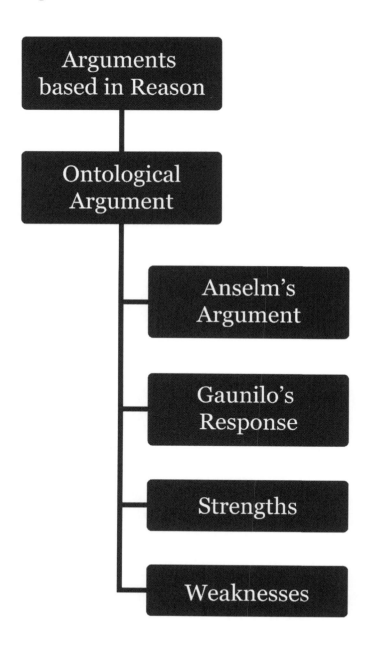

Arguments based in Reason

Ontological Argument

Anselm's Argument

Gaunilo's Response

Strengths

Weaknesses

The Ontological Argument

A. Anselm's Ontological Argument

The Fool – Proslogion Chapter 1

In chapter 1 of the Proslogion, Anselm reflects on the fool who says in his heart that there is no God. Anselm considers that the fool knows what God is and so is a fool for believing that God does not exist.

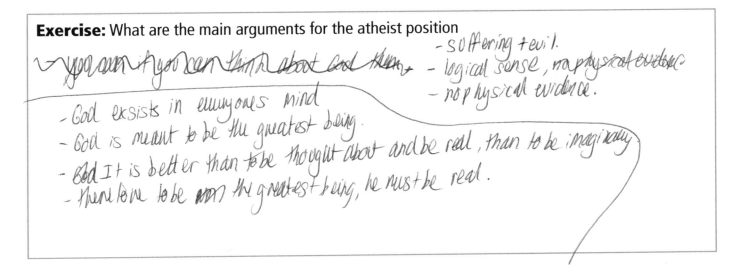

Exercise: What are the main arguments for the atheist position

- suffering + evil.
- logical sense, no physical evidence
- no physical evidence.

✓ you can if you can think about God then

- God exsists in everyones mind
- God is meant to be the greatest being.
- God It is better than to be thought about and be real, than to be imaginary
- therefore to be the greatest being, he must be real.

Version 1 – Proslogion Chapter 2

In Chapter 2 of the Proslogion, Anselm attempted to prove God existed analytically (prior to any evidence) that God must exist. His argument took this form:

Premise 1: God is a being than which nothing greater can be conceived.

Premise 2: It is greater to exist in the mind and reality than in the mind alone.

Premise 3: God must be a being that exists in the mind and reality otherwise God is not a being than which nothing greater can be conceived.

Conclusion: God exists.

Exercise : Explain each premise of the argument in Proslogion Chapter 2.

turn to previous pg.

The Painter – Proslogion Chapter 2

Anselm gave the example of the painter to emphasise premise 2:

For, it is one thing for an object to be in the understanding, and another to understand that the object exists. When a painter first conceives of what he will afterwards perform, he has it in his understanding, but be does not yet understand it to be, because he has not yet performed it. But after he has made the painting, be both has it in his understanding, and he understands that it exists, because he has made it. (Proslogion)

Exercise: Draw the painter with a blank canvas thinking about a painting and the painter with a complete canvas thinking about the painting his has just painted. Identify the second as the greater idea as it is a thought about an existing painting.

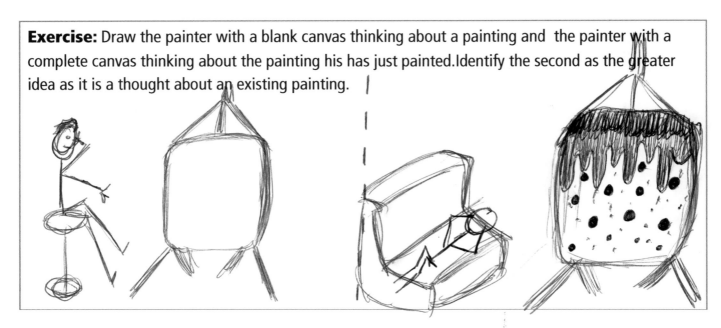

Version 2 – Proslogion Chapter 3

In chapter 2, Anselm gave a second version of the ontological argument:

Premise 1: God is a being than which nothing greater can be conceived.

Premise 2: It is greater to be a being that cannot be conceived not to exist than to be a being that can be conceived not to exist.

Premise 3: God must be a being that cannot be conceived not to exist.

Conclusion: God must exist

In this version, Anselm is considering the notion of necessary and contingent existence and categorising God as a necessary being as necessary existence is greater than contingent existence.

Exercise: Write a list of things that are contingent and the things that they need to exist. Start with yourself, e.g. you are contingent on the air you breathe and your parents etc.

me   → parents   Pencil - led
trees → seed   to wood ← to the
                           wood - wood chopper.

'Version 2 is the same as version 1'. Do you agree? Give reasons for and against this position.

For
- still saying God exsists in thought.
so thurefore must be real.

Against
- idea of necessity + contingency.
- God is necessary.

B. Gaunilo's Response

1. Understanding is not accepting – In Defence of the Fool

Gaunilo argued that one could understand Anselm's definition of God without accepting it as sound. There is a difference between valid and sound arguments. Just because an argument is valid, this does not make it sound (true). Just because we can agree on the logic of Anselm's argument, does not mean we accept it.

Exercise: Write a valid (logical) but unsound (not truthful) argument

logical to think that I could be a millionaire as
via inheritance.

2. The Rumour – In Defence of the Fool

Gaunilo argues that we can form ideas in our minds because we have general understandings in our minds of different things. He gives the example of the rumour.

Suppose that I should hear something said of a man absolutely unknown to me, of whose very existence I was unaware. Through that special or general knowledge by which I know what man is, or what men are, I could conceive of him also, according to the reality itself, which man is.

Exercise: Draw two cells. Label the first 'complex idea' and the second 'basic ideas'.

In the first cell draw a unicorn and Spongebob Squarepants. In the other, draw the elements that make up those two ideas. In the second cell describe what is being considered. In the other explain how we can conceive of the complex ideas because we already have basic ideas.

3. The Island – In Defence of the Fool

Gaunilo's famous example is that of the island. In this example, Gaunilo is arguing that you cannot define God into existence moving from the idea de dicto to assuming its existence in reality de re.

Now if someone should tell me that there is such an island, I should easily understand his words, in which there is no difficulty. But suppose that he went on to say, as if by a logical inference: "You can no longer doubt that this island which is more excellent than all lands exists somewhere, since you have no doubt that it is in your understanding. And since it is more excellent not to be in the understanding alone, but to exist both in the understanding and in reality, for this reason it must exist. For if it does not exist, any land which really exists will be more excellent than it; and so the island already understood by you to be more excellent will not be more excellent."

Exercise: What does it mean to say: you cannot go from de dicto to de re?

imaginary

reality.

(exsistence in) that mind

35

C. Kant's Challenges to the Ontological Argument

Existence is not a predicate – Transcendental Dialectic (Book II chapter III, Section 4)

Immanuel Kant's rejection of the Ontological Argument is based in his argument that existence is not a predicate. Anselm and Descartes after him assume that we can talk of God's existence as though it is a predicate of God. Anselm argues that God is that than which nothing greater can be conceived and so existence is particular to Him. Kant rejects this as we cannot speak of existence in the same way as of other predicates.

But if, on the other hand, we admit, as every reasonable person must, that all existential propositions are synthetic, how can we profess to maintain that the predicate of existence cannot be rejected without contradiction? (Immanuel Kant)

Exercise: What are the predicates of the following: grass, triangles, tables, cats?

green , 3 sides, Meow .

has to have a leg .

Identify something that cannot not exist, whose existence is necessary for the sake of other things (e.g. my parents cannot not exist if I exist). Now try to identify something that is necessary in itself.

Sun cannot not exist without the grass

S is P

Kant later argued the logical point that when we make statements about predicates they are always of the form S (subject) is P (predicate), e.g. grass is green, Lions are fierce etc. However, the statement 'God exists' is not of the form S is P and so existence cannot be a predicate.

Exercise: Formulate your own example of S is P and explain.

 the sky is blue.

D. Evaluating Anselm

St Thomas Aquinas

Aquinas argues that God's existence is self-evident to Himself, but not to us.

'God exists,' of itself is self-evident, for the predicate is the same as the subject, because God is His own existence as will be hereafter shown …Now because we do not know the essence of God, the proposition is not self-evidence to us; but needs to be demonstrated by things that are more known to us.

Exercise: Explain how Aquinas challenges the ontological argument in principle.

- ea dunt no evidence.

- exsist but only in imagination.

Alvin Plantinga

In God, Freedom and Evil, Plantinga responded to Gaunilo's Island challenge by making the point that when we talk of perfection we are not talking about contingent things. Only God can be perfect as only God can possess the intrinsic maxim of perfection.

No matter how great the island is, no matter how many Nubian maidens and dancing girls adorn it, there could always be a greater – one with twice as many for example. The qualities that make for greatness of an island … most of these qualities have no intrinsic maxim. …So the idea of a greatest possible island is an inconsistent idea; it's not possible that there be such a thing. (Alvin Plantinga)

Exercise: To what extent does Plantinga successfully challenge Gaunilo?

There can never be perfection as there can always be something better.

↑ logical idea.

Consider Normal Malcolm's suggestion that God is either impossible or necessary. What does that mean?

Russell and Instantiation

Russell argues the same point when he discusses instantiation. In order to discuss the qualities of anything, we must first instantiate it and then discover its properties. If we look at existence in this way we see that the statement 'God exists' tells us nothing as we must first instantiate God in order to see if He possesses the predicate of existence. However, once you have instantiated God you need not look for existence; alternatively if you cannot instantiate God you can never demonstrate God's existence.

Exercise: Consider Frege's example 'Tame tigers exist' and 'Tame tigers eat a lot'. Explain how one contains a predicate and the other does not.

Anselm's Fool – Proslogion Chapter III

Anselm considers God's existence to be self-evident by virtue of the fact that God is the greatest possible being. It is possible that Anselm is assuming the cosmological position that all things need a creator and God is that creator and so it is obvious that there cannot be a world without a creator. Alternatively, Anselm could be assuming the cosmological argument that the world is contingent and so depends on a necessary being.

Why, then, has the fool said in his heart, there is no God (Psalms xiv. 1), since it is so evident, to a rational mind, that you do exist in the highest degree of all? Why, except that he is dull and a fool?

Exercise: What does it mean to say that you believe that the world was created but that you do not believe in a creator?

See that the world was created but don't neccesaryly ned a creator e.g. big bang.

Anselm against Atheism

Another way of reading Anselm is from the position of a straight attack on atheism. Anselm is reflecting on the notion that if God exists, then God is transcendent and above all things. For an atheist to state with any kind of certainty that there is no God, would assume that somehow the atheist has a complete understanding of the nature of the universe and all existence. Anselm is therefore stating that anyone who speaks with certainty that there is no God, is a fool. It would be like burying my head in the ground and saying: I do not see the sun, so there is no sun.

Exercise: What does an atheist understand by the notion 'God'?

*don't believe in him
but can still think about him.*

To what extent does Anselm successfully disprove the atheist position (not necessarily proving the theistic position).

*— if Athiests can think about God and God is perfect
then he must exist.*

Essay Skills

Types of Questions

Questions on this topic might focus on Anselm's Ontological Argument directly or on the challenges of the argument. Whichever it asks, candidates should always use the other in evaluation. Some examples of questions you might be asked are these:

Question	What it is asking
Assess the claim that you can prove God analytically.	You need to explain Anselm's argument and emphasise that it is an analytic argument attempting to prove God's existence prior to experience.
Existence is not a predicate.' Discuss.	This question is focussed on Kant's rejection of the ontological argument. You should first outline the ontological argument so that you can tackle the assumption that existence is a predicate.
Anselm was wrong to suppose that God could be proven a priori.' Discuss.	You should outline Anselm's argument first and then you can use either Gaunilo or Kant to attack it. Make sure you evaluate both positions.
You cannot go from de dicto to de re.' Discuss.	This question is specifically referring to Gaunilo's challenge that you cannot define God into existence. Outline the Ontological Argument first, then explain Gaunilo's position.

Exercise: Analyse this question: Assess the claim that the ontological argument fails to prove that God exists a priori.

Essay skills – Balancing your Essay

When an examiner reads your essay they will know where you stand by your thesis statement. However, they will expect you to be able to argue and defend that position. If your essay is too biased without any attempt to present the opposite position, then it will lose marks for not being evaluative. On the contrary, if your essay has lots of arguments against your thesis statement but you conclude that way regardless, your essay will look weak as you have not resolved the problems and defended your position.

Exercise: Write your thesis statement and then write the outlining points of six paragraphs, three supporting your thesis statement and three against it. Make sure that the points for your thesis statement resolve the challenges that are raised in the statements against your thesis statement. For each point, identify a scholarly view that will justify it.

A Posteriori Arguments

Structure of Thought

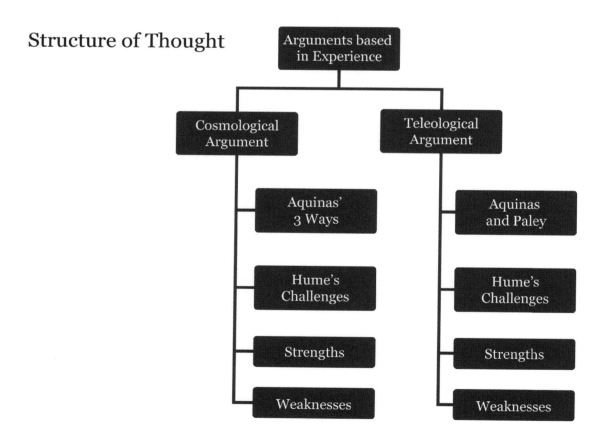

The Cosmological Argument

A. Aquinas' Cosmological Argument

Aquinas' First Way from motion – Summa Theologica

Aquinas' first way argues that all things are moving right now and that in order for them to be moving there must be a First Mover that is itself unmoving. Rather than see this as a chain of motion backwards in time, it is more a matter of sustenance. The First Mover is moving things right now. If there was no First Motion tomorrow, there would be no motion at all.

Premise 1: We experience motion, e.g. planets.

Premise 2: A thing cannot move itself, motion is the reduction of potentiality to actuality

Premise 3: Only something actually moving can move something potentially moving. E.g. the fire makes the potentially hot wood actually hot.

Premise 4: Infinite regression is impossible as without a first motion there would be no motion at all.

Premise 5: There must be an unmoved first mover.

Conclusion: This is what we call God.

For motion is nothing else than the reduction of something from potentiality to actuality. But nothing can be reduced from potentiality to actuality, except by something in a state of actuality. Thus that which is actually hot, as fire, makes wood, which is potentially hot, to be actually hot, and thereby moves and changes it.

Exercise: Explain how the argument from motion is a posteriori.

Aquinas' Second Way from Causation – Summa Theologica

Aquinas' second way considers the chain of cause and effect. While Aquinas was not explicitly discussing a chain of causation backwards in time, there is an inherent link between cause and effect and time. One thing causes another allowing it to then cause another.

Premise 1: We experience cause and effect, e.g. parents cause children.

Premise 2: A thing cannot cause itself, e.g. a child cannot be its own parent.

Premise 3: Only a prior event can cause a later effect; this is a chain of cause and effect.

Premise 4: Infinite regression is impossible as there would be no first cause.

Premise 5: There must be a first caused which is itself uncaused.

Conclusion: This is what we call God.

Now in efficient causes it is not possible to go on to infinity, because in all efficient causes following in order, the first is the cause of the intermediate cause, and the intermediate is the cause of the ultimate cause, whether the intermediate cause be several, or only one. Now to take away the cause is to take away the effect. (Summa Theologica)

Exercise: How is this argument of causation linked to Aristotle's argument of four causes?

Peter Kreeft explained cause and effect in terms of existence being a gift being passed down a chain. He gave the example of a book being passed on from one person to another. However, if it never came into existence in the first place it can never pass on to you. Research Peter Kreeft's Thomist (Thomas Aquinas') Cosmological Argument online. Summarise his example.

Aquinas' Third Way from Contingency and Necessity – Summa Theologica

Aquinas' third way from contingency and necessity considers time to be infinite. This being the case, every possibility would have played out, including the possibility that there was nothing in existence at all. Since every contingent thing needs to be brought into existence, there must be something that is itself necessary.

Premise 1: We experience things that are not necessary to exist.

Premise 2: A thing that is contingent cannot explain itself.

Premise 3: There must be a necessary thing to bring about a contingent one.

Premise 4: Infinite regression is impossible as you have not explained anything.

Premise 5: There must be a necessary being.

Conclusion: This is what we call God.

Therefore we cannot but postulate the existence of some being having of itself its own necessity, and not receiving it from another, but rather causing in others their necessity. This all men speak of as God. (Summa Theologica)

Exercise: Peter Kreeft summarised this argument by appealing to the pre-Big Bang theory notion of Steady State theory that if there has already been an infinite amount of time, then every possibility has already been actualised. This being the case everything in existence can cease to be. Explain how the Third Way attempts to prove there must be a necessary being.

Draw a mind-map with God in the centre and three paths leading to God. On each path closest to God, write 'that which we call God'. At the start of each path, start writing the premises of each argument building towards the centre.

B. David Hume's Challenges

1. Infinite Regression

David Hume argues that the notion of infinite regression is not a contradiction and is theoretically acceptable. For this reason the need for a first mover is unnecessary. Many classical and modern scientists have theorised that the universe is infinite with not actual beginning.

Exercise: Peter Kreeft commented that when Fr George Lemaitre first presented the Big Bang theory it was criticised by atheist scientists as being camouflaged theism. In what way does Aquinas' First Mover echo biblical ideas of creation.

2. Need for a Sufficient Reason – Dialogues Concerning Natural Religion

David Hume challenges the need for a First cause by undermining the notion that Gottfried Leibniz lobbied, that there needs to be a sufficient reason or, as Aquinas calls it, a First Cause.

"The WHOLE, you say, wants a cause. I answer, that the uniting of these parts into a whole, like the uniting of several distinct counties into one kingdom, or several distinct members into one body, is performed merely by an arbitrary act of mind, and has no influence on the nature of things. Did I show you the particular cause of each individual in a collection of twenty particles of matter, I should think it very unreasonable, should you afterwards ask me, what was the cause of the whole twenty. This is sufficiently explained in explaining the cause of the parts." (Dialogues)

Exercise: What is a sufficient reason? Why is it unnecessary, according to Hume?

3. Cause and Effect

David Hume argues that all assertions about the nature of cause and effect are based in observation and without observation we cannot make assumptions. Since we cannot speak about the causes of universes from experience, we can never speak about the cause of the universe as being God. His example of the billiard balls suggest that we cannot infer knowledge of the motion of X from the motion of Y as the two motions are completely different.

"But to convince us that all the laws of nature, and all the operations of bodies without exception, are known only by experience, the following reflections may, perhaps, suffice. Were any object presented to us, and were we required to pronounce concerning the effect, which will result from

it, without consulting past observation, after what manner, I beseech you, must the mind proceed in this operation? ... For the effect is totally different from the cause, and consequently can never be discovered in it. Motion in the second billiard ball is a quite distinct event from the motion in the first. Nor is there anything in the one to suggest the smallest hint of the other." (David Hume)

Exercise: William of Ockham first presented the challenge against the cosmological argument on the basis that we cannot experience cause and effect. Research this challenge.

Explain how Hume's challenge echoes William of Ockham's challenge to Aquinas.

---

4. Need for a Necessary Being – Dialogues Concerning Natural Religion

David Hume challenges the notion that we can ever talk about God as necessary being. He argues that no existence can be considered necessary.

"There is an evident absurdity in pretending to demonstrate a matter of fact, or to prove it by arguments a priori. Nothing is demonstrable, unless the contrary is a contradiction. Nothing, that is directly conceivable, implies a contradiction. Whatever we conceive as existent, we can also conceive as non-existent. There is no being, therefore, whose non-existence implies a contradiction. Consequently there is no Being whose contradiction is demonstrable." (David Hume)

Exercise: Explain the similarities and differences between Hume's argument and here and Kant's argument against the Ontological Argument.

C. Evaluating the Cosmological Argument

Kant's challenge of cause and effect – Transcendental Dialectic

Kant argues that our understanding of cause and effect only applies in this world where we can experience it. Outside of this universe (from whence the universe comes) we cannot speak about cause and effect in any sensible way.

We find, for instance, (1) the transcendental principle whereby from the contingent we infer a cause. This principle is applicable only in the sensible world; outside that world it has no meaning whatsoever. For the mere intellectual concept of the contingent cannot give rise to any synthetic proposition, such as that of causality. The principle of causality has no meaning and no criterion for its application save only in the sensible world. But in the cosmological proof it is precisely in order to enable us to advance beyond the sensible world that it is employed. (Immanuel Kant)

Exercise: Explain what Kant means by 'this principle is applicable only in the sensible world.'

Copleston's Argument from Contingency – BBC Radio Debate 1948

In the radio debate between Bertrand Russell and Friedrich Copleston, Copleston presents the argument from contingency where he appeals to the need for a sufficient reason to explain all things:

We know that there are at least some beings in the world which do not contain in themselves the reason for their existence. For example, I depend on my parents, and now on the air, and on food, and so on.

Now, secondly, the world is simply the real or imagined totality or aggregate of individual objects, none of which contain in themselves alone the reason of their existence. There isn't any world distinct from the objects which form it, any more than the human race is something apart from the members.

Therefore, I should say, since objects or events exist, and since no object of experience contains within itself the reason of its existence, this reason, the totality of objects, must have a reason external to itself. And that reason must be an existent being. Well, this being is either itself the reason for its own existence, or it is not. If it is, well and good. If not, then we must proceed further.

But if we proceed to infinity in that sense, then there's no explanation of existence at all. So, I should say, in order to explain existence, we must come to a Being which contains within itself the reason for its own existence, that is to say, which cannot not exist.

Exercise: Paragraph 1: Give examples of necessary and contingent things.

Paragraph 2: What does Copleston mean when he says the world is an 'aggregate of individual objects, none of which contain in themselves alone the reason for their existence?

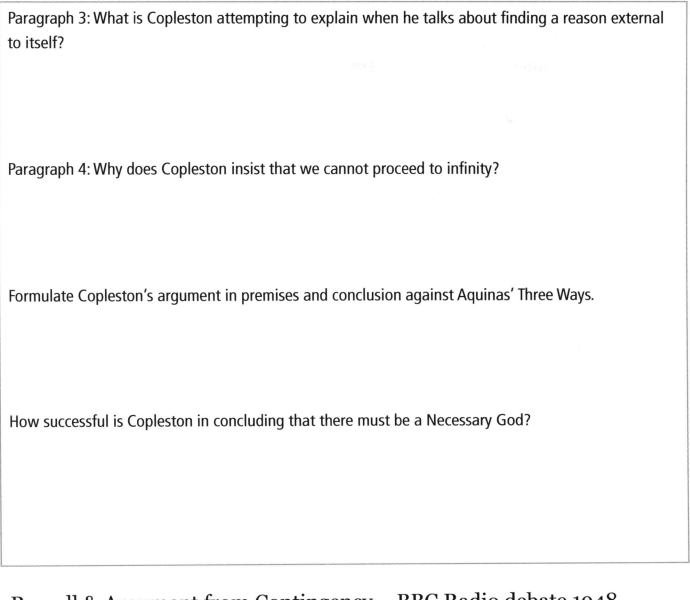

Paragraph 3: What is Copleston attempting to explain when he talks about finding a reason external to itself?

Paragraph 4: Why does Copleston insist that we cannot proceed to infinity?

Formulate Copleston's argument in premises and conclusion against Aquinas' Three Ways.

How successful is Copleston in concluding that there must be a Necessary God?

Russell & Argument from Contingency – BBC Radio debate 1948

Bertrand Russell's rejection of Copleston's argument rests on the semantics Copleston is using, specifically the world 'necessary'.

The word "necessary" I should maintain, can only be applied significantly to propositions. And, in fact, only to such as are analytic -- that is to say -- such as it is self-contradictory to deny. I could only admit a Necessary Being if there were a being whose existence it is self-contradictory to deny. I should like to know whether you would accept Leibniz's division of propositions into truths of reason and truths of fact. The former -- the truths of reason -- being necessary. (Bertrand Russell)

The Teleological Argument

A. Aquinas' Teleological Argument

Aquinas' Fifth Way – Summa Theologica

In the Fifth Way, Aquinas appeals to the governance of the world. He observes a posteriori that things move in accordance to a pre-existing law towards their purposes. In this way, the Fifth Way is a qua regularity teleological argument. Additionally, Aquinas argues that all things have a pre-existing purpose towards which they are directed. In this way, the Fifth Way is a qua purpose teleological argument.

Purpose – Summa Theologica

Aquinas argues that all things move towards their purpose in order to flourish. He is echoing Aristotle who argued that all things have a telos.

The fifth way is the governance of the world. We see that things which lack intelligence, such as natural bodies, act for an end, and this is evident from their acting always, or nearly always, in the same way, so as to obtain the best result. Hence it is plain that not fortuitously, but designedly, do they achieve their end. (Thomas Aquinas)

Exercise: What does Aquinas mean by things that lack intelligence moving towards their ends?

The Archer – Summa Theologica

Aquinas argued that only things with intelligence can move themselves towards their purposes. Things without intelligence need to be moved.

Now whatever lacks intelligence cannot move towards an end, unless it be directed by some being endowed with knowledge and intelligence; as the arrow is shot to its mark by the archer.

Exercise: Draw an archer loosing an arrow towards a target. Label what is happening in accordance with Aquinas' analogy.

Supreme Intelligence – Summa Theologica

Therefore some intelligent being exists by whom all natural things are directed to their end; and this being we call God. (Thomas Aquinas)

Exercise: How does Aquinas conclude that God exists?

In what way is Aquinas' conclusion that there is a God in the Fifth Way similar to his conclusion that there is a God in the First to Third Ways?

B. William Paley's Teleological Argument

Natural Theology

William Paley wrote Natural Theology in which he described his observations of the world and the order that appeared within it. Based on his observations he argued that all things were fit for purpose, in that they were all 'designed' perfectly to do what they did. In this way Paley's is a qua purpose teleological argument.

Fit for Purpose

Paley gave various examples in Natural Theology of things that appear in the natural world that are fit for purpose: the duck's webbed feet, the swan's long neck, the pig's multiple teats, the human eye etc.

The Watch analogy – Natural Theology

Paley give his famous example of the watch to emphasise how the watch, being complex, needs a watchmaker, and so the world, being more complex than the watch, needs a designer also.

Suppose I pitched my foot against a stone and were asked how the stone came to be there, I might possibly answer that for anything I knew to the contrary it had lain there forever. But suppose I had found a watch upon the ground, and it should be inquired how the watch happened to be in that place, I should hardly think of the answer which I had before given, that for anything I knew the watch might have always been there.

This mechanism being observed the inference we think is inevitable, that the watch must have had a maker-that there must have existed, at some time and at some place or other, an artificer or artificers who formed it for the purpose which we find it actually to answer, who comprehended its construction and designed its use. (William Paley)

Exercise: How useful is Paley's analogy in helping us understand the need for a designer?

What does Paley mean by an artificer or artificers?

C. David Hume's Challenges

The Voice of Cleanthes – Dialogues Concerning Natural Religion

David Hume wrote Dialogues Concerning Natural Religion in which he deals with teleological arguments 23 years before Paley, so was not responding to him. In his work, Hume creates a dialogue between fictitious characters (similar to Plato). The voice of the theist is Cleanthes and the voice of the sceptic (Hume himself) is Philo. Cleanthes makes his case for God:

'Look around the world, contemplate the whole and every part of it: you will find it to be nothing but one great machine, subdivided into an infinite number of lesser machines.'

Exercise: What analogy does Cleanthes make about the world?

In what way is Cleanthes' example similar to Paley's later example?

Formation of the Argument

Cleanthes' argument can be formulated in this way:

Premise 1. In the same way that a machine needs a designer, the world also needs a designer.

Premise 2. A great design necessarily implies Greatness in the designer.

Premise 3. There is clearly great design in the world.

Conclusion. There must be a great designer of the world.

Exercise: Write the formation of Cleanthes argument and leave spaces next to it for Paley's version and for responses to the premises.

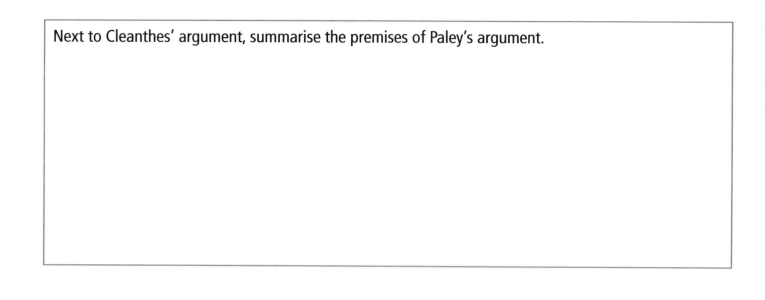

Next to Cleanthes' argument, summarise the premises of Paley's argument.

Hume's Argument against Premise 1

Hume argues that the teleological argument attempts to draw an analogy between the world and something that is evidently designed. He argues that analogy is limited in strength unless the two things being compared are similar. He was famed for stating that the world is more like a cabbage than a machine.

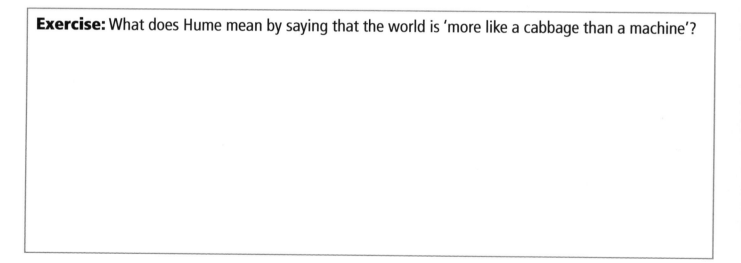

Exercise: What does Hume mean by saying that the world is 'more like a cabbage than a machine'?

Hume's Argument against Premise 2

Hume attacks the implication that the world is perfectly designed. He comments that nature is 'red in tooth and claw'. If the nature of the designer can be seen in the creation, it follows, then that the designer of this world is itself malevolent or imbecilic.

Hume's Argument against Premise 3

Hume challenges the idea that we can assume that there is design in the world. He attacks this from the logical position that A B does not imply B A. For example, while it may be the case that 'if it is raining I will be carrying an umbrella' it does not follow that 'if I am carrying an umbrella then it is raining'.

Hume argues that we cannot assume that there is design just because there is apparent design. If we cannot experience the designer then we cannot speak of design.

While we can experience the minds behind designed and directed things in the world we experience, we cannot assume there is a mind behind the world as we have no possible experience of such a mind. We cannot compare temporal things with the universe itself.

Alternatives to Apparent Design

Hume offers alternatives to the existence of apparent design in the world:

i)   Matter and energy may well be everlasting.

ii)   An infinite number of combinations of the world are possible

iii)   Once order has occurred, it will tend to perpetuate itself.

iv)   Perpetuated order appears as design.

Exercise: Explain how modern explanations for the universe including evolution, inflation and multiverse can be identified with Hume's alternatives to explain apparent design.

D. Evaluating the Teleological Argument

Mill on the Evils of Nature – On Nature

John Stuart Mill argued that there could not be a good designer God on the basis that there was so much suffering in nature.

Next to taking life (equal to it according to a high authority) is taking the means by which we live; and Nature does this too on the largest scale and with the most callous indifference. A single hurricane destroys the hopes of a season; a flight of locusts, or an inundation, desolates a district; a trifling chemical change in an edible root starves a million people. ...Everything, in short, which the worst men commit either against life or property, is perpetrated on a larger scale by natural agents. (John Stuart Mill)

Exercise: How convincing is Mills' challenge to a designer God?

Research Richard Dawkins' example of the digger wasp and explain how it supports Mill's argument of the evils of nature.

Richard Swinburne's Challenge to Aquinas – The Existence of God

Swinburne points out that Aquinas commits the circular reasoning fallacy. He assumes that the world is designed in order to conclude that there is a designer.

Aquinas' statement that all things are directed by some mind towards a purpose and that mind is God commits the fallacy of begging the question. Things need a purpose, God gives things a purpose, therefore God must be the purpose.

Exercise: What is the fallacy of circular reasoning?

The teleological argument also commits the fallacy of induction. What is this?

Richard Dawkins against Paley – The Blind Watchmaker

Richard Dawkins responds directly to William Paley arguing that in fact things are not fit for purpose, but that any apparent design is the effects of evolution, not a designer God.

Paley's argument is made with passionate sincerity and is informed by the best biological scholarship of the day, but it is wrong, gloriously and utterly wrong. The analogy between the telescope and eye, between watch and living organism, is false. All appearances to the contrary, the only watchmaker in nature is the blind force of physics, albeit deployed in a special way. (Richard Dawkins)

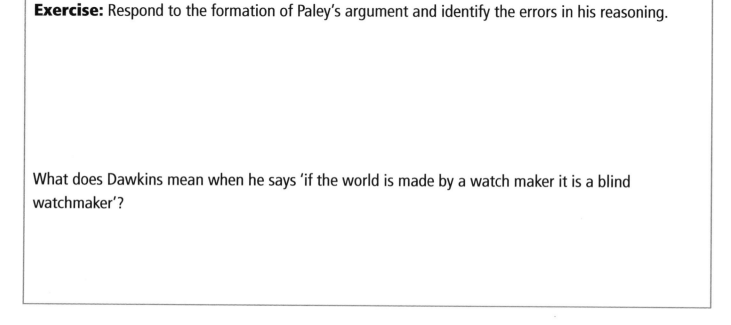

Exercise: Respond to the formation of Paley's argument and identify the errors in his reasoning.

What does Dawkins mean when he says 'if the world is made by a watch maker it is a blind watchmaker'?

Irreducible Complexity – Dawkins' Black Box

Michael Behe presented the defence for intelligent design by presenting examples of organisms which, he argued, could not have evolved over time because their complexity could not be reduced or simplified.

By irreducible complexity I mean a single system which is composed of several interacting parts that contribute to the basic function, and where the removal of any one of the parts causes the system to effectively cease functioning. (Michael Behe)

Behe responded to a point that Darwin made in Origin of Species:

'If it could be demonstrated that any complex organ existed which could not possibly have been formed by numerous, successive, slight modifications, my theory would absolutely break down.'

Exercise: Research examples that Behe's considers irreducibly complex: The Bacterial Flagellum, the Cilium, the ATP Synthase Molecule.

Research William Dembski's Specified Complexity. How does Specified Complexity support the belief in intelligent design?

Essay Skills

Types of questions

Questions on this topic might focus on the Cosmological Argument, the Teleological Argument, a posteriori arguments in general or the challenges to one or both of the arguments. If the question is specifically about the Cosmological or Teleological Argument, candidates should not discuss the other argument. However, if the question is about a posteriori arguments, candidates should mention both. Candidates should always evaluate using Hume's relevant challenges.

Question	What it is asking
Assess the claim that the world needs a First Cause.	This question is asking about the cosmological argument and specifically the second way. Candidates should focus on the second way, fully analysing it, focussing on all premises. You should evaluate with Hume's challenges.
Evaluate Hume's challenges of the cosmological argument.	This question is specifically focussed on Hume's challenges of the cosmological argument. You should outline Aquinas' three ways, and then critically examine them with Hume's challenges.
The existence of design proves that there must be a God.' Discuss.	This question is about the design argument in general. You should outline Aquinas' and Paley's versions emphasising the design and fit for purpose aspects of each and then evaluate with Hume and any other appropriate arguments.
A posteriori arguments fail to prove that there is a God.' Discuss.	This question is about a posteriori arguments in general, not the cosmological or teleological alone. You should outline the main arguments of each before evaluating. Focus on one line of reasoning in the cosmological argument, and then move onto teleological arguments. Pick Hume's main challenge against each.

Exercise: Analyse this question: To what extent can you prove God exists a posteriori.

Essay Skills – Knowing what to Include and Omit

There is so much information that can be used in any essay one of the difficulties is knowing what to include and what to leave out. This can be a daunting task and can lead candidates to spend far too long on one essay and then not have enough time on other questions. In order to overcome this, you need to know what is relevant and only include that. This is called selection of relevant material.

Knowing what to leave out is just as important as knowing what to include as putting in too much can 1) cost you time and 2) take the essay off track.

Take the question above: To what extent can you prove God exists a posteriori. This is a prime example of there being too much information to include into a 40 minute essay.

Exercise: Write the essay title at the top of this page and draw two columns. In one column write down the points you want to include, (e.g. Aquinas' 1st Way, Paley's Watch, Hume's fallacy of analogy), and in the other column write down the points that you don't want to include (e.g. Copleston's argument from contingency, Behe's irreducible Complexity).

God and the World

Religious Experience

Structure of Thought

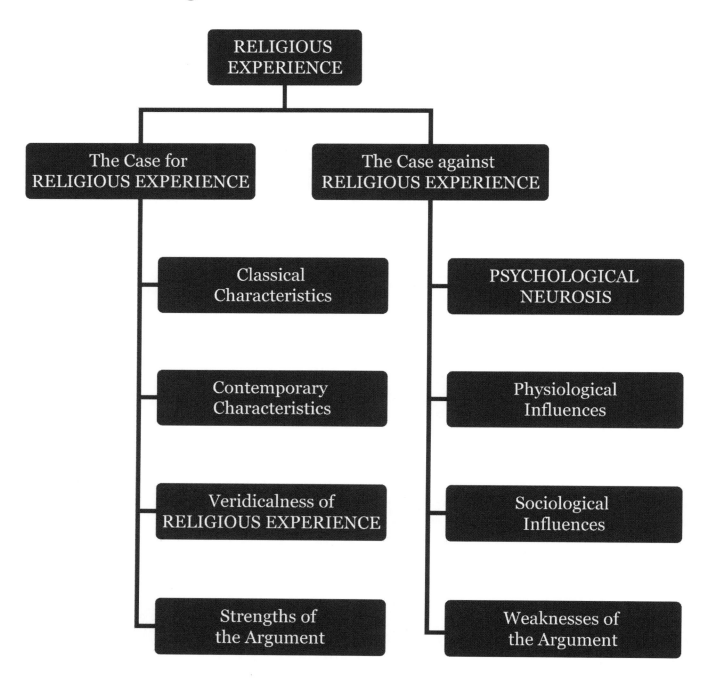

The Case for Religious Experience

A. Classical Characteristics

Types of Religious Experiences

We find examples of religious experiences in the Bible and contemporary accounts by mystics – people who receive religious experiences within Christian tradition. Religious experiences are either direct revelations of God or indirect realisations of the nature of God and our relationship with Him. They appear as either voices or visions. Each type of religious experience shares similar characteristics.

Voices

Voice experiences share three characteristics: Disembodied, Noetic and Authoritative.

Moses and the Burning Bush – Exodus 3:2-10
2 The angel of the LORD appeared to Moses in flames of fire from within a bush. Moses saw that though the bush was on fire it did not burn up. 4 When the LORD saw that he had gone over to look, God called to him from within the bush, "Moses! Moses!" And Moses said, "Here I am." 5 "Do not come any closer," God said. "Take off your sandals, for the place where you are standing is holy ground." 6 Then he said, "I am the God of your father,[a] the God of Abraham, the God of Isaac and the God of Jacob." At this, Moses hid his face, because he was afraid to look at God. 7 The LORD said, "I have indeed seen the misery of my people in Egypt. I have heard them crying out because of their slave drivers, and I am concerned about their suffering. 10 So now, go. I am sending you to Pharaoh to bring my people the Israelites out of Egypt."

The Conversion of Saul – Acts 9:3-6
3 Now as Saul journeyed he approached Damascus, and suddenly a light from heaven flashed about him. 4 And he fell to the ground and heard a voice saying to him, "Saul, Saul, why do you persecute me?" 5 And he said, "Who are you, Lord?" And he said, "I am Jesus, whom you are persecuting; 6 but rise and enter the city, and you will be told what you are to do."

Exercise: Define the three characteristics of voice experiences.

Identify the three characteristics as they appear in the account of Saul's conversion.

Visions

There are three types of vision experiences: intellectual, corporeal and imaginative.

St Bernadette's vision of Mary
"I came back towards the grotto … I had hardly taken off the first stocking when I heard a sound like a gust of wind. … As I raised my head to look at the grotto, I saw a Lady dressed in white, wearing a white dress, a blue girdle and a yellow rose on each foot, the same colour as the chain of her rosary; the beads of the rosary were white."

Joseph's Dream – Genesis 37: 5-11
5 Joseph had a dream, and when he told it to his brothers, they hated him all the more. 6 He said to them, "Listen to this dream I had: 7 We were binding sheaves of grain out in the field when suddenly my sheaf rose and stood upright, while your sheaves gathered around mine and bowed down to it."

St Teresa of Avila's vision of Jesus – Autobiography of Teresa of Avila
I was at prayer on a festival of the glorious Saint Peter when I saw Christ at my side -- or, to put it better, I was conscious of Him, for neither with the eyes of the body nor with those of the soul did I see anything. I thought He was quite close to me and I saw that it was He Who, as I thought, was

speaking to me. …All the time Jesus Christ seemed to be beside me, but, as this was not an imaginary vision, I could not discern in what form: what I felt very clearly was that all the time He was at my right hand, and a witness of everything that I was doing, and that, whenever I became slightly recollected or was not greatly distracted, I could not but be aware of His nearness to me.

Exercise: Define the three types of vision experiences.

Identify the type vision Teresa of Avila experienced and explain why it is this type.

Corporate Religious Experiences

A corporate religious experience is one that is shared by many people at the same time.

Pentecost – Acts 2:1-4
2 When the day of Pentecost had come, they were all together in one place. 2 And suddenly from heaven there came a sound like the rush of a violent wind, and it filled the entire house where they were sitting. 3 Divided tongues, as of fire, appeared among them, and a tongue rested on each of them. 4 All of them were filled with the Holy Spirit and began to speak in other languages, as the Spirit gave them ability.

Draw a circle with 8 segments from the centre. Label one segment 'types of religious experiences'. Label the other 7: Disembodied, noetic, authoritative, intellectual, corporeal, imaginative, and corporate. In each segment: a) define it and b) give an example of it.

B. Contemporary Characteristics

William James

William James was a psychologist who investigated several examples of religious experiences and identified four characteristics that were common: Passive, Ineffable, Noetic and Transient.

The Case of S. H. Hadley – Varieties of Religious Experience
"One Tuesday evening I sat in a saloon in Harlem, a homeless, friendless, dying drunkard. I had pawned or sold everything that would bring a drink. I had often said, 'I will never be a tramp, I will find a home in the bottom of the river.' As I sat thinking, I seemed to feel some great and mighty

presence. I did learn afterwards that it was Jesus, the sinner's friend. I went to the nearest station-house and had myself locked up. The following Sabbath I went to Jerry McAuley's Mission. There was a sincerity about this man that carried conviction, and I found myself saying, 'Dear Jesus, can you help me?' Never with mortal tongue can I describe that moment, I felt the glorious brightness of the noonday sun shine into my heart. I felt I was a free man."

The Case of an Oxford Graduate – Varieties of Religious Experience
"Between leaving Oxford and my conversion I never darkened the door of my father's church, although I lived with him for eight years, sometimes drunk for a week together. I was converted in my own bedroom at precisely three o'clock in the afternoon of a hot July day, having been off the drink for a month. A young lady friend had sent me Professor Drummond's 'Natural Law'. 'He that hath the Son hath life eternal, he that hath not the Son hath not life' I had read scores of times before, but this made all the difference. I had the feeling that there was another being in my bedroom, the stillness was marvellous, and I felt supremely happy. But the day after my conversion I went to lend a hand with the harvest, and came home drunk. My poor sister said I had fallen away instantly. But I knew that God's work begun. About midday I made on my knees the first prayer before God for twenty years. From that hour I have never wanted drink. The same thing occurred with my pipe: after being a regular smoker from my twelfth year the desire for it went at once, and has never returned."

Exercise: Define the terms: Passive, Ineffable, Noetic and Transient.

Explain how the four characteristics appear in the case of S. H. Hadley.

Richard Swinburne

Richard Swinburne characterises religious experiences into the following categories: Public ordinary, public extraordinary, private describable, private non-describable, private non-specific.

The Transfiguration – Matthew 17:1-8

17 Six days later, Jesus took with him Peter and James and his brother John and led them up a high mountain, by themselves. 2 And he was transfigured before them, and his face shone like the sun, and his clothes became dazzling white. 3 Suddenly there appeared to them Moses and Elijah, talking with him. 4 Then Peter said to Jesus, "Lord, it is good for us to be here; if you wish, I will make three dwellings here, one for you, one for Moses, and one for Elijah." 5 While he was still speaking, suddenly a bright cloud overshadowed them, and from the cloud a voice said, "This is my Son, the Beloved; with him I am well pleased; listen to him!" 6 When the disciples heard this, they fell to the ground and were overcome by fear. 7 But Jesus came and touched them, saying, "Get up and do not be afraid." 8 And when they looked up, they saw no one except Jesus himself alone.

St Thomas Aquinas' First Way – Summa Theologica

The first and more manifest way is the argument from motion. It is certain, and evident to our senses, that in the world some things are in motion. … Therefore it is necessary to arrive at a first mover, put in motion by no other; and this everyone understands to be God.

The Case of Stephen H Bradley – Varieties of Religious Experience

I began to feel my heart beat very quick all on a sudden, which made me at first think that perhaps something is going to ail me, though I was not alarmed, for I felt no pain. My heard increased in its beating, which soon convinced me that it was the Holy Spirit from the effect it had on me. I began to feel exceedingly happy and humble, and such a sense of unworthiness as I never felt before. … a stream (resembling air in feeling) came into my mouth and hear in a more sensible manner than that of drinking anything, which continued, as near as I could judge, five minutes or more, which appeared to be the cause of such a palpitation in my heart.

The Ecstasy of Teresa of Avila – The Autobiography of Teresa of Avila

It pleased the Lord that I should sometimes see the following vision. I would see beside me, on my left hand, an angel in bodily form -- a type of vision which I am not in the habit of seeing, except very rarely. Though I often see representations of angels, my visions of them are of the type which I first mentioned. It pleased the Lord that I should see this angel in the following way. He was not tall, but short, and very beautiful, his face so aflame that he appeared to be one of the highest types of angel who seem to be all afire. They must be those who are called cherubim.

Exercise: Define each of Swinburne's characteristics of religious experiences.

Identify which of Swinburne's categories is represented by the Transfiguration and explain why this is the case.

C. Veridicalness (truthfulness) of Religious Experience

William James on Authority

In On Authority, Lecture XVI and XVII on Mysticism, William James describes religious experiences as being psychological but emphasises the authority they have over recipients. He separates the recipient from the rationalists who grumble about the experience. The mystic having received the experience is the one who knows the truth of their experience.

As a matter of psychological fact, mystical states of a well-pronounced and emphatic sort are usually authoritative over those who have them. They have been 'there,' and know. It is vain for rationalism to grumble about this. If the mystical truth that comes to a man proves to be a force that he can live by, what mandate have we of the majority to order him to live in another way? We can throw him into a prison or a madhouse, but we cannot change his mind — we commonly attach it only the more stubbornly to its beliefs. (William James)

Exercise: Identify an example of a religious experience that had authority over the recipient and affected their lives in a substantial way (you can use an example from this study guide).

Why might J. L. Mackie complain and say that if a person knows the psychological nature religious experiences and still accepts that they have authority, then they are 'insufficiently critical'?

Why might William James argue that a religious experience is 'psychological' but still argue that it has authority?

Richard Swinburne on Credulity and Testimony

Richard Swinburne argued that there are two principles which defend the authority of the religious experience: the Principles of Credulity and Testimony.

What seems to you to be so on the basis of experience, probably is so- in the absence of counter-evidence. …What people tell you is probably true- in the absence of counter-evidence. (Richard Swinburne)

Under what conditions might a person consider their experience was NOT a genuine religious experience?

Why is it so important we acknowledge the Principle of Testimony?

Anthony O'Hear

Anthony O'Hear postulated that religious experiences caused problems because they were uncheckable. Whenever we experience anything we always check them:

1. Over time

2. With other senses

3. With other checkers

The problem with religious experiences is that they cannot be checked in the same way. This makes them uncheckable.

Exercise: What does it mean to say a statement is checkable?

Why are religious experiences different from other kinds of experiences?

The Case against Religious Experience

A. The Psychological Challenge

Dr Persinger

The psychological challenge against religious experience is that all experiences originate in the brain. Dr Persinger argued that all experiences were brain experiences and argued that religious experiences may well be 'miss-firings of the brain.' He did research on the 'God-helmet' which bombards the temporal lobes with magnetism in order to induce 'religious' experiences which can then be compared to 'authentic' mystical experiences.

Ben Shermer is part of the sceptics' movement and argues that while religious experiences are real, they are not external events but rather internal events. This being the case, religious experiences are not genuine religious experiences as they have no external source.

Exercise: What is meant by 'miss-firings of the brain'?

What is the purpose of the God-helmet?

Sigmund Freud

In The Future of an Illusion, Sigmund Freud argued that religion was itself a psychological neurosis. In which case religious experience, as a by-product, has no authentic value.

Religion is comparable to a childhood neurosis. Our knowledge of the historical worth of certain religious doctrines increases our respect for them, but does not invalidate our proposal that they should cease to be put forward as the reasons for the precepts of civilization.

Thought point: The Future of an Illusion is mentioned in the ethics syllabus under conscience. Freud's argument is that conscience is formed in early childhood by parental praise and blame. He calls this the superego - a source of irrational guilt and neurosis.

Exercise: What does it meant to call religion a neurosis?

How does undermining the authenticity of religion undermine religious experiences?

Timothy Leary

Timothy Leary conducted studies in the 1960s comparing accounts of 'religious experiences' with accounts of those having consumed hallucinogens. The accounts were indistinguishable.

Huston Smith, in Do Drugs have Religious Import?, commented on the distinction between these types of experiences. While the accounts may be similar, the long term effects on a person taking hallucinogens is vastly different from the long term effects on a person who claims to have had a 'religious experience.'

Drugs appear able to induce religious experiences; it is less evident that they can produce religious lives. It follows that religion is more than religious experiences.

Exercise: How might Leary's studies undermine religious experiences?

How might Smith's argument defend the authority of religious experience despite the psychological challenge?

B. The Physiological Challenge

The Case of Phineas Gage

In Harlow's account of Phineas Gage, he was described as a well-liked, happy and competent foreman who suffered the tragedy of having a metal pole through his head. After this experience, part of the pole was removed but part remained. He went from being happy to angry and competent to not being able to do his job at all.

This case study shows us how the brain and actions that affect the brain affect our characters and our experiences. Therefore, if the brain can be physiological affected through health etc. it affects our experiences.

Exercise: Research his experience and note the significant points

---

Physical Health

The physiological challenge is that physiological problems and health problems etc. cause the brain to create or interpret experiences in a particular way that they appear as religious experiences. In this way, the physiology of the person affects the way their psyche interprets experiences.

This might explain why many of the mystics, Teresa of Avila, Bernadette of Soubirous, Julian of Norwich etc. were very sick, often on their deathbed. Perhaps their experiences were induces by their sickness, perhaps by the medication they took.

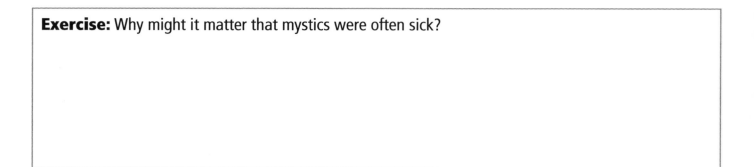

Exercise: Why might it matter that mystics were often sick?

Landsborough

Landsborough argued that St Paul may well have been epileptic, and that his blindness may have been caused by the epilepsy affecting his temporal lobes. While there is no certain proof of this, it would undermine the authority of his conversion on the road to Damascus as it may have been the by-product of stress and his medical condition.

Exercise: How might St Paul's conversion be otherwise explained?

Stern disagreed with Landsborough's conclusions arguing that there was no way that we could ascertain whether or not St Paul had temporal lobe epilepsy based on a few passing comments. To what degree is Stern right?

C. The Sociological Challenge

Karl Marx

The sociological challenge is presented by the work of Karl Marx and suggests that all things influence our minds and behaviour, including our society. This being the case, it is no wonder that Christians see visions of Mary and Hindus of Vishnu. We are conditioned by our societies to want to see things in a certain way.

Marx argued that religion was the 'opium of the masses' and that religion was a construct which oppressed the people. For this reason it was suspect and so any experiences that a person received would have been part of the form of social control over the people.

Exercise: What is the sociological challenge?

Why did Karl Marx call religion the 'opium of the masses'?

How does the sociological challenge seek to undermine the authority of religious experiences?

"A person's religious experience is conditioned by their culture in the same way that a dream is always translated into a person's language. This does not make it false." Discuss. M

Essay Skills

Types of Questions

Questions on this topic might focus on the William James or Richard Swinburne directly, or perhaps on one or more of the types of religious experiences. Alternatively, the question might focus on the challenges to religious experiences. There are many avenues that an examiner might take to assess a candidate's knowledge on this topic. Candidates should remember to include the arguments for religious experiences as well as evaluating against it. There must be a sense of dialogue between the two positions.

Question	What it is asking
Critically analyse the conclusions drawn by William James in Varieties of Religious experience.	Here you need to look at what James argues about religious and mystical experiences, including the four characteristics, and particularly evaluate his position that religious experiences are psychological experiences.
Assess the claim that voice experiences are nothing more than the mind.	You need to give examples of voice experiences, their characteristics and then consider how they can be explained from a psychological perspective.
Religious experiences are neurosis.	This is a psychological challenge essay. You need to present the case for experiences before presenting the challenges posed. Remember to try to respond to these challenges but know your thesis statement and keep it balanced.
Religious experiences are the best argument that God musts exist	This question is asking about how genuine religious experiences are for the recipients particularly and whether or not we can use their experiences as evidence for the rest of us that there is a God.

Exercise: Analyse this question: 'Religious experiences are psychological experiences.' Discuss.

Essay Skills – Hooks at the Start of your Paragraphs

Each paragraph needs to stand by itself and tell a part of the overall essay, but they must also work together as a constant train of thought. One way to make sure that all paragraphs feel like they are part of the same essay is to use hooks which connect the paragraph to the previous paragraph and signpost why this paragraph is being mentioned at all.

Examples of good hooks are:

William James wrote about his research into religious experiences in Varieties of Religious Experiences.	This hook makes clear who this paragraph will be about and mentions their main work.
In response, Richard Swinburne presented his principles of Credulity and Testimony.	This hook shows that the paragraph comes right after the previous one for a reason, as Swinburne will respond to whatever challenge was just raised.
Freud challenged the notion of religion which in turn undermines religious experience.	This hook attempts to move the essay in a different direction having introduced Freud to the essay.

Exercise 2: Look at an essay you have written on religious experiences and write hooks for each paragraph. Then take the essay title from **exercise 1** and write hooks for five paragraphs you would write.

The Problem of Evil and Suffering

Structure of Thought

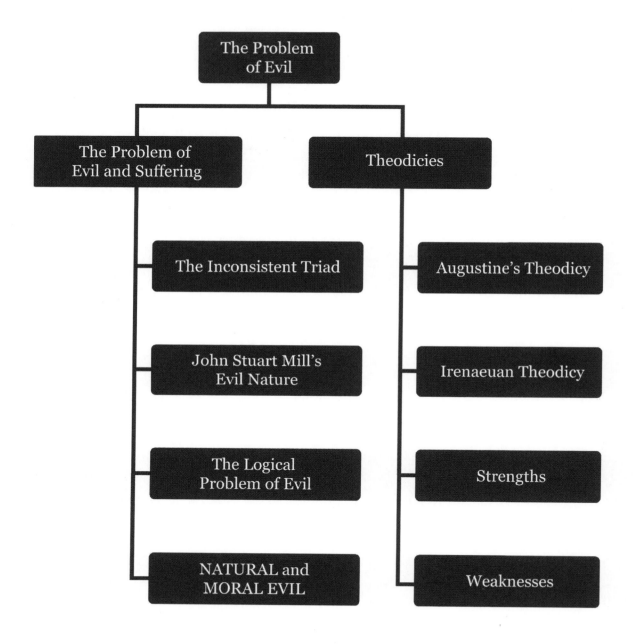

The Problem

A. The Inconsistent Triad

Attributes of God

God is seen to be omnipotent and benevolent within scripture and revelation. In theophany events of the Bible we see God's actions and call Him powerful and loving. For example the creation story is attributed to an all-powerful God and the incarnation of Christ to die for mankind is attributed to an all-loving God. This being the case, we see God as being omnipotent and benevolent.

Exercise: What does omnipotent mean?

all powerful

What does omnibenevolent mean?

all loving

Suffering

The existence of suffering is seen by Hans Küng as the rock of atheism. Peterson (1998) considered it a form of moral protest against God. If God existed, why would he allow suffering in the world? More recently, Stephen Fry called God a maniac for allowing such suffering as bone cancer in children when he could easily prevent it.

Exercise: What is meant by the 'rock of atheism'?

why would he allowed suffering, base and core argument.

Why is the problem of evil a form of moral protest?

why would God to this to us.

What does Fry mean when he calls God a maniac?

allowing and causing people to suffer
↑ madness.

Epicurus

Epicurus formulated the problem of evil in his inconsistent Triad where he articulated that God could not be both all loving and all powerful if there was evil and suffering in the world. This was further articulated by David Hume.

Is God willing to stop evil but not able? Then he is impotent.

Is God able to stop evil but not willing? Then he is malevolent.

Is God willing and able? The whence cometh evil?

Is God neither willing nor able? Then why call him God?

Exercise: What is meant by the 'inconsistent triad'?

omnipotent
doesn't at add up.
evil exsists
all loving.

Why is God's omnipotence and benevolence not compatible with the existence of suffering?

- if God is unable to stop suffering then he is not all powerful.
- if he is able but chooses not to then he is all loving.

B. John Stuart Mill's Evil Nature

John Stuart Mill

John Stuart Mill complained that the idea that there is a benevolent designer God was incompatible with the evidence we have of the world. In On Nature, he comments that the evils that nature commits would be condemnable were they to be committed by human beings. This being the case we cannot conclude that it was created by a sane and benevolent designer.

Nearly all the things which men are hanged or imprisoned for doing to one another are nature's everyday performances. Even the love of 'order', which is thought to be a following of the ways of nature, is in fact a contradiction of them. All which people are accustomed to deprecate as 'disorder' and its consequences, is precisely a counterpart of nature's ways. Anarchy and the reign of Terror are overmatched in injustice, ruin, and death by a hurricane and a pestilence. Not even on the most distorted and contracted theory of good which was ever framed by religious or philosophical fanaticism, can the government of nature be made to resemble the work of a being at once good and omnipotent. (John Stuart Mill)

Exercise: What does Mill mean when he calls 'disorder' a counterpart to 'nature's ways'?

→ nature should follow a law of order.

→ therefore when human nature follows disorder it goes against this.

What does Mill mean when he says that no moral theory can make the 'the government of nature...at once good and omnipotent'?

→ no theory can combat this issue and show God to be loving.

Richard Dawkins

In support of Mill's attack on God on the basis of the cruelty of nature and in line with Fry's attack on God, Richard Dawkins refers to the reproductive habits of digger wasps who paralyse prey, such as caterpillars, in order to inject their larvae inside them to incubate before exploding out. This cruelty in nature, Dawkins argues, is characteristic of the blind forces of nature and can never be attributed to any foresight by a benevolent God.

Exercise: In what way does the digger wasp example show that there cannot be a loving God?

how could a loving God cause his creature to endure such suffering.

C. The Logical Problem of Evil

Mackie against Theism

J. L. Mackie challenged theism in The Miracle of Theism but arguing that there is no rational basis for religious beliefs. He argued that several aspects were inconsistent with each other. The notion of God being both loving and powerful is testament to this contradiction as God cannot both be able and willing to stop evil and at the same time choose not to do so.

Here it can be shown, not that religious beliefs lack rational support, but that they are positively irrational, that several parts of the essential theological doctrine are inconsistent with one another.

Exercise: What does Mackie mean when he says that religious beliefs are irrational?

irrational as it does not make any logical sense and instead is full on contradiction.

The Logical Problem

Mackie and McCloskey together presented the logical problem of evil where they considered all characteristics of God:

1. God is omnipotent

2. God is benevolent

3. God is omniscient

They argued that these attributes combined form a logical contradiction with the existence of evil and suffering in the world. By this argument, it is irrational to believe in God as to do so would be to support a logical contradiction.

Exercise: What does it mean to call God omniscient?

all knowing .

How is it a logical contradiction to call God omnipotent, benevolent and omniscient and still there be evil and suffering in the world?

if he can't stop evil - not omniscient + non omnipotent
but if he can and doesn't = not benevolent .

D. Natural and Moral Evil

Peter Vardy's Types of Natural Evil

Peter Vardy argued that there were five types of natural evil and suffering?

1.   The suffering caused by natural disasters.

2.   The suffering caused by diseases.

3.   The suffering caused by the inadequacy of the human body.

4.   The suffering caused by mental health.

5.   The suffering of animals.

These five types of suffering are not accountable by human actions as they are occur naturally and so it is not enough to claim free will causes suffering as the vast majority of suffering we endure in the world is caused by natural origins.

Exercise: Draw a five segment circle and label each one with one of the five types of natural evil.

Hebblethwaite's Natural and Moral Evil

Hebblethwaite argued that what we call moral evil and suffering is in fact a form of natural evil and suffering. This can be seen in two ways:

1.   The moral decisions to cause suffering occurs naturally within us.

2.   Our physiology that allows us to feel moral suffering is a natural physiology.

By this argument, Hebblethwaite argued that moral evil was in fact natural evil and cannot be accounted for by human free will.

Exercise: What does Hebblethwaite mean when he says that moral evil and suffering is natural evil and suffering?

Theodicies

A. Augustine's Theodicy

The Problem of Evil

St Augustine considered evil a problem on the following basis:

Premise 1. God created all things.

Premise 2. Evil is a thing.

Conclusion. God created evil.

St Augustine relied on the truth of Genesis (though not literal truth of the creation story as Augustine was NOT a creationist) to show that all things came from God. This being the case, evil things need accounting as God, who is good, cannot be the author of evil things.

And I said, Behold God, and behold what God has created; and God is good, yea, most mightily and incomparably better than all these; but yet He, who is good, has created them good, and behold how He encircles and fills them. Where, then, is evil, and whence, and how crept it in hither? What is its root, and what its seed? Or has it no being at all? Why, then, do we fear and shun that which has no being? (Confessions, Book 7 Chapter 5)

The Literal Meaning of Genesis

Perhaps Sacred Scripture in its customary style is speaking with the limitations of human language in addressing men of limited understanding. ... The narrative of the inspired writer brings the matter down to the capacity of children.

Exercise: What is the problem of evil for St Augustine?

Why does Augustine talk about evil as if it is something separate from God's creation?

believe it is not a direct result of action which God wanted.

Evil as Privation

Augustine used the term 'privation' to describe evil. He distinguished between two types of privation, that which we cannot help, e.g. not having the ability to breathe under water, and that which we can help, e.g. not helping the poor etc. Augustine said that things are evil when they are deprived of their goodness, so a person is evil when he is emptied of good and his actions are not actions that he should be performing.

Therefore, if they shall be deprived of all good, they shall no longer be. So long, therefore, as they are, they are good; therefore whatsoever is, is good. That evil, then, which I sought whence it was, is not any substance; for were it a substance, it would be good. For either it would be an incorruptible substance, and so a chief good, or a corruptible substance, which unless it were good it could not be corrupted. I perceived, therefore, and it was made clear to me, that Thou made all things good, nor is there any substance at all that was not made by You; and because all that You have made are not equal, therefore all things are; because individually they are good, and altogether very good, because our God made all things very good. (Confessions, Book 7 Chapter 12)

This can be seen reflected in Herbert McCabe's example where he says we can all recognise broken deckchairs and sour grapes. They are deprived of their goodness and so they are bad as they do not live up to their expectations. We can see this echoing Aristotle's telos and Plato's notion of the Essential FORM of goodness bringing goodness to all things.

Exercise: What are the two type of privation?

(1) One which we cannot help

(2) One which we can help.

What does it mean to call a person 'depraved'?

things are only evil when deprived of goodness.

Freewill Defence

Alvin Plantinga presented the free will defence where he argued that in order for God to create perfectly free human beings, it was necessary that he create us with the capacity to do evil actions, otherwise we would be holy robots and not free at all. This supports Augustine's theodicy as Augustine calls upon the story of The Fall and shows how this illustrates human disobedience. This disobedience is our free will choice to do things God does not want. This is what brings about evil and suffering.

Exercise: What is the Free Will defence?

Hierarchy of Creation

Augustine's theodicy concerning free will and disobedience is not limited to human action. Augustine postulated that angels and demons were also free will agents with the capacity to disobey God. This disobedience causes the natural evil that we experience in the world.

For a pre-scientific society that had no understanding of medicine and tectonic plate movement, etc. this was a viable explanation for the existence of evil and suffering caused by nature. However, this is not an adequate explanation now as we know better than to look to spiritual entities for the explanations of natural phenomena.

Exercise: What is the hierarchy of creation?

How are spiritual beings linked to the existence of human suffering?

Alternate Reading of Augustine

While not explicitly the Augustinian theodicy, there is another way we can explain natural evil and suffering from an Augustinian perspective. Augustine makes it clear that evil is not a thing in itself, but an absence of good, so when we see suffering in nature we can immediately look at it differently and recognise that there is in fact no evil going on. Animals cannot be evil to each other, so natural suffering is not evil. Evil is the moral conscious decision to disobey God. Nature does not consciously disobey God, this includes death and disease etc. It may not be how things are designed to be but there is no conscious moral decision to disobey.

Secondly, the association between evil and suffering is an artificial association linked to the hedonistic principle articulated by Jeremy Bentham when he said that we are under the governance of pleasure and pain. The notion that things that cause suffering are bad/evil is part of a hedonistic worldview. Many pleasurable things are bad and many painful things are good. (Without toothache our teeth would rot away - pain is the warning signal). Therefore, to argue that there is natural evil in the world is an utter misunderstanding born of disobedience to the will of God.

Weaknesses of Augustine

Friedrich Schleiermacher argued that there is a logical contradiction in the idea of a perfect world going wrong which is what appears to be the case with the hierarchy of creation and the disobedience of man. If God is omniscient, He should have known that mankind would disobey Him. Therefore, whether or not we have free will, God is still accountable for the suffering as He was aware of it when He created the world. Indeed, the fact that God creates hell is indication that God knew the world would go 'wrong'.

It seems a matter of semantics to say that evil is not a thing, it's just the decisions people make. Goodness is not a thing either, it is just something that happens. Either evil happens or it does not. If it does happen then it could have not happened. If God was benevolent and omnipotent he would have been able to prevent it from happening.

Exercise: What is Schleiermacher's contradiction?

How does God's omniscience escalate the problem?

B. Hick's Theodicy

Image and Likeness

John Hick's theodicy is based on St Irenaeus'. Irenaeus was a Creationist, not that this influences the working of the theodicy. Irenaeus argued that God created all human beings in His image, but not His likeness. By this, he meant that we are created in the embryonic form of God. We are in God's image (we have reason and morality etc.) but we are not yet like God. In the same way that children are born in their parents' image but are not yet grown to be like them.

In Evil and the Love of God, Hick echoed Irenaeus - it is our job on earth to grow in the likeness of God through our actions and decisions. In this way, suffering is necessary to help us grow and learn. Without suffering we could not learn at all.

Instead of regarding man as having been created by God in a finished state, as a finitely perfect being fulfilling the divine intention for our human level of existence, and then falling disastrously away from this account sees man as still in process of creation. (John Hick)

Exercise: In what way is Hick's theodicy an Irenaean theodicy?

Write out Genesis 1:26. What does Hick think this verse means?

Soul-Making

Irenaeus thought that the story of the creation and fall of mankind as one example of the relationship between God and human beings. While Irenaeus was a creationist, it was irrelevant to the working of the theodicy. Adam and Eve were the first examples of what happens when we disobey God. We are punished and through that punishment we grow. Therefore, suffering is a

Hick maintained this notion and considered the struggle of life on earth as the journey we take from child-like innocence to the reflection of the likeness of God. This second stage of the creative process, becoming like God, is not a process that can be performed by God, but rather one that has to be performed by the willingness of the individual. That said, as we are made at an epistemic distance from God, it is not a journey we can do alone.

By this 'likeness' Irenaeus means something more than personal existence as such; he means a certain valuable quality of personal life which reflects finitely the divine life. This represents the perfecting of man, the fulfilment of God's purpose for humanity, the 'bringing of many sons to glory', the creating of 'children of God' who are 'fellow heirs with Christ' of his glory.' (John Hick)

Exercise: Draw Adam and Eve. Label them with all the child-like qualities they might have had.

How might this child-like innocence have led them to disobeying God?

What does Hick mean when he says we must become 'fellow heirs with Christ'?

Not Paradise

Hick wanted to maintain that the attitude that God cannot exist because there is suffering in the world is a mistaken one. This is not meant to be a paradise but instead a place of learning and growth. We cannot learn if there are no consequences to our actions and no risk to our decisions. For this reason, suffering is necessary and God is not morally accountable for this suffering. It is part of the perfect world God created for the purpose of helping us be more like Him.

Critics are confusing what heaven ought to be, as an environment for perfected finite beings, with what this world ought to be, as an environment for beings who are in process of becoming perfected. For if our general conception of God's purpose is correct the world is not intended to be a paradise, but rather the scene of a history in which human personality may be formed towards the pattern of Christ. Men are not to be thought of on the analogy of animal pets, whose life is to be made as agreeable as possible, but rather on the analogy of human children, who are to grow to adulthood in an environment whose primary and overriding purpose is not immediate pleasure but the realizing of the most valuable potentialities of human personality. (John Hick)

Exercise: What attitude is the mistaken attitude?

Imagine a perfect world. What would it be like?

How might Alvin Plantinga's challenge of Gaunilo's perfect island be useful in responding to this perfect world image?

Model of Christ

Hick postulated that Christ's is the image and likeness of God and that we should attempt to emulate Him. Christ is our connection with God and the model of how we should behave.

Following hints from St. Paul, Irenaeus taught that a man has been made as a person in the image of God but has not yet been brought as a free and responsible agent into the finite likeness of God, which is revealed in Christ.

Exercise: Why is Christ such an important figure?

In what way is Christ the image and likeness of God (Nicene creed 'true God of true God"?

Weaknesses of Hick

Hick's argument that, eschatologically (at the end of time), we will all be saved, is problematic as it is a contradiction of all Christian attitudes about heaven and hell. Further, if all will be saved in the end, it makes all moral decision making on earth utterly pointless.

Further, the idea that God creates suffering in the world to test us seems rather malevolent. Testing should be fair giving the people undergoing the test a chance of passing and certainly a sense where they understand they are being tested. For babies to die, people in third world countries to live in poverty etc. all for the sake of 'testing us', seems utterly malevolent and cruel rather than loving.

Exercise: What is problematic about the notion that everything will be resolved eschatologically?

How might universal salvation be considered by some to be unchristian?

Why is the idea of God testing us immoral?

Why might Gottfried Leibniz call this be best of all possible worlds is there is so much intended suffering in it?

Essay Skills

Types of Questions

Questions on this topic might focus on the Problem of Evil itself, which would require you to evaluate its threat using theodicies or it may ask you about one or both theodicy directly. Candidates should remember that if they are asked about Augustine's theodicy, they may not need to mention Hick's theodicy at all and vice versa. It is also important to note that a question about Hick is not asking about Irenaeus, but since Hick's theodicy is based on Irenaeus' it is not a problem to mention the association so long as the focus is on Hick.

Question	What it is asking
The problem of evil cannot be resolved.' Discuss.	This question is asking you to explain the problem of evil and suffering and show how Augustine's and Hick's theodicy attempt to resolve it.
Assess the extent to which Augustine successfully resolves the problem of evil and suffering.	You need to present the problem of evil and suffering first, and then assess Augustine's theodicy. You do not need to mention Hick's theodicy here.
Hick's theodicy is too farfetched to be true.' Discuss.	You need to present the problem of evil and suffering first, and then assess Hick's theodicy and how farfetched or likely it is. You do not need to mention Augustine's theodicy here.
Evaluate the claim that Augustine's theodicy is the best attempt at resolving the problem of evil and suffering.	You need to present the problem of evil and suffering first. You then need to assess Augustine's theodicy and then compare it directly with Hick's to show which is better.

Exercise: Analyse this question: "Assess the extent to which the problem of evil and suffering proves there cannot be a God".

» Augustine.

Essay Skills – Citing scholars

In your essay you need to show your knowledge and understanding of the different arguments and the scholars that present them. It is important to note that the essay is not so much your opinions and ideas that you are presenting but your understanding of other people's ideas. For this reason it is important to make good use of scholarly views and opinions and make it clear that you understand how they compare with each other.

Your first paragraph should be focused on one main argument. This will usually, though not always, be the argument presented by one particular scholar, e.g. cosmological argument is presented by Aquinas, the theory of FORMs is Plato's. However, the problem of evil and suffering is no one scholar's view, so you would need to present a number of scholarly ideas in that first paragraph. However, you should make sure that one scholar leads the argument, e.g. for the problem of evil it is Epicurus or Hume and other thinkers support that initial argument, e.g. Mill and Dawkins etc.

Each paragraph should be effectively one scholarly perspective supported by others. In this way, think of your scholars as either primary or secondary scholars. Primary scholars in the question of the problem of evil are: Epicurus/Hume, Augustine and Hick. Secondary scholars are Mill, Dawkins, Peterson, Irenaeus etc. By identifying scholars as primary and secondary you can then start thinking who is the main scholar of each paragraph and how can you support them with other scholars.

It is also important not to just name drop: "Augustine was supported by Plantinga…" and "Hick's ideas were good but they were challenged by Dawkins…" You need to make it clear that you understand how these other scholars support and challenge. E.g. Augustine's argument that human disobedience is what causes suffering is supported by Plantinga's Free Will Defence which places all accountability on human free will which necessarily permits us to do evil otherwise we cannot be truly free" and "Hick's idea that suffering is necessary is convincing but does not respond to Dawkins' presentation of the suffering that takes place in nature, such as the digger wasp's paralysing of the caterpillar, since an omnipotent God could easily have created an alternative model." You need to make it clear that you understand the scholar's view and can use them properly.

Exercise: Take the question in the previous exercise on page 103. Identify what your five paragraphs will be for your essay. Pick a leading scholar for each paragraph and at least one support scholar for each. Write a sentence for each paragraph where you back up or challenge a main scholar with a secondary scholar.

Nature of God

Classical Attributes of God

Structure of Thought

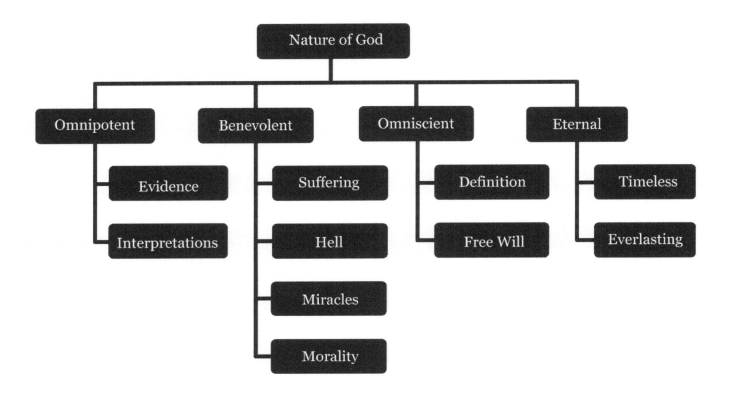

Omnipotence

A. Interpretations of God's Omnipotence

God Can Do the Logically Impossible

René Descartes was a mathematician and in Meditations postulated that God, being omnipotent, was not bound by out mathematical laws. Therefore, God could do even what appears to be logically impossible to us. God is not limited by our understanding of the logically possible.

God is the sum of all perfections; he can do anything, including what might seem impossible. For example, God could change the fundamental laws of physics, which as far as we know are unchangeable and apply universally. God can do anything, including what might seem impossible. For example, God could change the fundamental laws of physics, which as far as we know are unchangeable and apply universally. God is the sum of all perfections. (Descartes)

Exercise: Write some examples of things that are logically impossible. E.g. making square circles.

Why would Descartes believe that God could do the logically impossible?

God Can Do the Logically Possible for God to Do

In Summa Theologica, St Thomas Aquinas postulated that God's omnipotence did not allow for Him to do the logically impossible, e.g. sin, die, climb trees etc. For this reason, God's omnipotence is limited to what God can logically do.

God cannot sin because this is a contradiction to the Nature of God as being good. In this way, it is illogical to speak of God climbing a tree, or creating an unliftable stone since God has no body with which to do it. God's Power can do anything. Whatever involves a contradiction is not held by omnipotence, for it just cannot possibly make sense of being possible ... For a contradiction in terms cannot be a world, for no mind can conceive it. (Aquinas)

Aquinas is supported by St Anselm who, in Proslogion, defined God as a being than which nothing Greater can be conceived.

God's nature is that than which nothing greater can be conceived God's existence is necessary attribute of God's nature. God is eternal because nothing can contain God. To speak of God sinning would be to see God as losing control over his actions, which is illogical since it would mean God is not omnipotent. (Anselm)

Exercise: What does Aquinas mean when he states 'anything that holds a contradiction cannot be help by omnipotence'?

Write a list of things that God could not logically do by this argument.

Omnipotence is a Statement of God's Power

A propositional interpretation of the Bible demands that we accept all statements in the Bible to be of equal literal meaning. When it states that God stopped the sun in the sky, we must read this as literal.

A non-propositional interpretation of the Bible demands that we take what is written as a symbol, metaphor or representation of the ideas and beliefs of the people who wrote it; not as literal.

Taking the Bible as non-propositional, we are left with no clear explanation of how we discuss God's omnipotence. God performs actions – theophany events – and we interpret them, sometimes as miracle events, other times as revelation. To call God omnipotent then is to state that God's actions go beyond ours but are not measurable in any way.

Thought Point: In the Christian Thought paper, Religious Pluralism suggest many different approaches to Christian faith. The literalists take a propositional approach tot eh Bible - these are sometimes labelled "Conservative Evangelical" or (misleadingly, as they take a certain hermeneutical view of the Bible) "Bible-believing Christians". For an explanation, read the Chicago statement on Biblical Inerrancy (1978).

Exercise: What is meant by a propositional interpretation of the Bible?

Give an example of a non-propositional interpretation the following Bible passage:

God created the world in six days and rested on the seventh.

B. God's Omnipotence Revealed

Biblical Revelation

We see evidence that God is omnipotent in various theophany events in the Bible, from the creation story to the story of the Flood. Particular miraculous acts in the Old Testament and the actions of Jesus Christ in the New Testament testify to the belief that God is omnipotent.

Exercise: Take one theophany from the Old Testament and one from the New Testament which demonstrate God's omnipotence. Explain how God's omnipotence is shown through this event.

Theophany events in the Old Testament	Theophany events in the New Testament
The Creation story (Genesis)	Jesus Christ' conception
The Flood (Genesis)	The turning of water into wine at Cana
The parting of the Red Sea (Exodus)	The calming of the storm
The halting of the sun in the sky (Joshua)	The healing of the paralysed man
The writing on the wall (Daniel)	The resurrection of Jesus Christ

---

Examples of God's Omnipotence in the Bible

God's omnipotence is revealed throughout the Old Testament through the actions that He performs, either through theophany events or through miracles.

In the beginning when God created the heavens and the earth … God said let there be light, and there was light. (Genesis 1:1)

The LORD threw down huge stones from heaven on them as far as Azekah, and they died … And the sun stood still, and the moon stopped, until the nation took vengeance on their enemies. (Joshua 10)

Greek Philosophical Thought

Plato theorised the existence of the Essential FORM of Goodness which gave life to all FORMs. The Neo-Platonist Plotinus identified this Essential FORM of Goodness with the creator God which he called 'The One'. The Essential FORM of Goodness is what gives life to all other FORMs and allows them to exist. Thus, it is the source of all life.

Aristotle theorised the existence of the Prime Mover which was pure act and the telos of all things. Aristotle postulated that the Prime Mover must be unchanging as it cannot improve as it cannot change. It is what allows any action to take place in the universe and it is what draws all things to itself.

List all the characteristics of the Prime Mover.

Benevolence

A. Human Suffering

God's Benevolence

O give thanks to the Lord, for he is good; steadfast love endures forever! (Psalm 118)

God loved the world that he gave his only Son, that whoever believes in him shall have eternal life. John 3

Exercise: What does Psalms 118 suggest about God's benevolence?

What does John 3 suggest about God's benevolence?

The Challenge of Human Suffering

The problem of evil and suffering is a direct challenge to the benevolence of God. If God was all loving, then it seems contradictory that God would allow suffering in the world.

Exercise: Define Omnipotent, Benevolent and Evil.

Outline how the Inconsistent Triad attempts to show God cannot exist.

The Theodicies

St Augustine's and John Hick's theodicies attempt to justify God in the face of suffering. Augustine's attempts to do this by showing that suffering is caused by disobedience, moral evil caused by humans and natural evil caused by demons. Hick's theodicy attempts to show that suffering is part of God's plan, that we should follow the example of Jesus and that ultimately God sill save all of us.

Exercise: Write one sentence explaining how St Augustine's theodicy responds to the problem of moral evil and suffering.

Write one sentence explaining how John Hick's theodicy responds to the problem of natural evil and suffering.

The Category Error of Evil and Suffering

One alternative way of looking at human suffering is by recognising that it is a naturalistic fallacy to think that just because suffering does occur that it is in fact evil. Further, the notion that [pleasure = good] and [pain = bad] is Jeremy Bentham's hedonistic principle. This is not necessarily demonstrative of the nature of good and evil and so just because suffering does happen, this does not mean that it is bad.

Exercise: Define 'naturalistic Fallacy'.

Explain how interpreting suffering as evil commits the naturalistic fallacy.

B. The Existence of Hell

The Challenge of Hell

The teaching of hell within the New Testament and Christian tradition is well documented and seems plain that God condemns to hell those who disobey Him and break His commandments. Hell is eternal damnation, visually represented as fire and suffering. The notion that a loving God would ever condemn any human being to an eternity of suffering for the sins committed in a human life seems contradictory.

45 Then he will answer them, 'Truly I tell you, just as you did not do it to one of the least of these, you did not do it to me.' 46 And these will go away into eternal punishment, but the righteous into eternal life." (Matthew 25:45-46)

22 The poor man died and was carried away by the angels to be with Abraham. The rich man also died and was buried. 23 In Hades, where he was being tormented, he looked up and saw Abraham far away with Lazarus by his side. 24 He called out, 'Father Abraham, have mercy on me...' 25 But Abraham said, 'Child, remember that during your lifetime you received your good things, and Lazarus in like manner evil things; but now he is comforted here, and you are in agony. 26 Besides all this, between you and us a great chasm has been fixed, so that those who might want to pass from here to you cannot do so, and no one can cross from there to us.' (Luke 16:22-26)

Exercise: What is the punishment for not showing love to the 'least of these'?

What happened to the rich man who did not show mercy to the poor man?

The Church's Teaching about Hell

The Catholic Church has never declared that any person is in hell, though it holds the belief that hell is the punishment for those who die in mortal sin. If God is love and human beings have free will, then it is necessary that God allows human beings to choose to reject Him and that rejection is hell.

The chief punishment of hell is eternal separation from God, in whom alone man can possess the life and happiness for which he was created and for which he longs. (Catechism of the Catholic Church 1035)

Exercise: Why may hell be a necessary teaching for a loving God?

What did C.S. Lewis mean when he said: 'the door to hell is locked from the inside'?

C. The Existence of Miracles

The Challenge of Miracles

If God is all loving, then it would be unfair for God to allow miracles to happen for some and not for others. In God's Action in the World, Maurice Wiles argued that miracles cannot possibly happen as it would show God to be flippant and partisan if he were to take action and save the Israelites from Slavery in Egypt but do nothing for the Jews in Auschwitz.

If the direct action of God, independent of secondary causation, is an intelligible concept, then it would appear to have been sparingly and strangely used. …It would seem strange that no miraculous intervention prevented Auschwitz or Hiroshima… Thus to acknowledge even the possibility of miracle raises acute problems for theodicy. The whole of creation is one creative act; God doesn't act repeatedly after this, it would show God to be flippant and partisan. (Maurice Wiles)

Further, Wiles argues that miracle events that the Church claims when canonising saints, may seem trivial in comparison to the need for divine intervention in times of crisis, e.g. war.

Exercise: List three miracles that take place in the Bible showing God's love for human beings.

Why does Wiles state that God would be flippant and partisan if He performed miracles for some and not others?

A Non-Propositional Reading of Miracles

One way of responding to this challenge is to change the way we read revelation in the Bible. If we read it as propositional then we are forced to justify partisan actions. If we read it as non-propositional, then we are able to interpret meaning.

Exercise: How might changing the way we read the Bible save God from being seen as flippant?

How might changing our understanding of a miracle as an act of wonder (miraculum) rather than as a nature defying event change the way we see miracles?

D. Morality

Euthyphro's Dilemma

In Euthyphro, Socrates challenges Euthyphro with this riddle: 'Is the pious loved by the gods because it is pious, or is it pious because it is loved by the gods?'

Horn 1: The pious is loved by the gods because it is pious.

Horn 2: The pious is pious because it is loved by the gods.

Exercise: What is the problem with accepting horn 1 of the argument?

What is the problem with accepting horn 2 of the argument?

Euthyphro's Dilemma as a Dilemma for Morality

This problem raises the question of whether or not God's commands are the source of morality or whether they are subject to an objective morality that is apart from God.

13 You shall not murder. 14 You shall not commit adultery. 15 You shall not steal. (Exodus 20: 13-15)

Now go and attack Amalek, and utterly destroy all that they have; do not spare them, but kill both man and woman, child and infant, ox and sheep, camel and donkey.'" (1 Samuel 15:3)

Exercise: What is the problem with accepting that God is not the source of morality? What becomes of God's commands in the Bible?

The Sacrifice of Isaac

The story of the sacrifice of Isaac causes problems for the question of morality. God commands Abraham to kill his only son to show his faith in God. However, when Abraham is about to go through with it, God stops him.

Immanuel Kant's response to the Sacrifice of Isaac:

There are certain cases in which a man can be convinced that it cannot be God whose voice he thinks he hears; when the voice commands him to do what is opposed to moral law, though the phenomenon seems to him ever so majestic and surpassing the whole of nature, he must count it a deception. (Immanuel Kant)

Exercise: How do the two horns of Euthyphro's dilemma appear in the story of Isaac's sacrifice?

According to Kant what did Abraham think God was commanding?

Here is the Jerome Bible Commentary on Kant's response:

The story is a masterpiece, presenting God as the Lord whose demands are absolute, whose will is inscrutable, and whose final word is grace. ...Such a Western argument [from Kant] reduces the climactic encounter between God and Abraham to an extrinsic moral debate.

Exercise: What does the final comment mean - 'an extrinsic moral debate'?

Goodness as a Reflection of God's Nature

Euthyphro's problem is only a problem is you categorise goodness and God as separate things. From a Christian theological perspective, this is a category error. Goodness is God-ness as Goodness is a reflection of God's nature – love.

Exercise: Plotinus identified the Essential FORM of Goodness with God. How does that resolve Euthyphro's dilemma?

Aristotle stated that the Prime Mover was perfectly Good, if the Prime Mover is God, how does this resolve Euthyphro's' dilemma?

God is Love

Christian theology demands that God is love. This being the case, any command is a command of love. So when God makes commands, they are commands of love. Further, since God is love, God can never make a command that is contrary to love.

7 *Beloved, let us love one another, for love is from God, and whoever loves has been born of God and knows God.* **8** *Anyone who does not love does not know God, because God is love. (1 John 4: 7-8)*

Exercise: What is the solution to Euthyphro's dilemma from the perspective that God is love?

4.1 Essay Skills

Types of Questions

Questions on this topic might focus on God's omnipotence or benevolence or philosophical problems raised with God's attributes. Depending on how the question is phrased, candidates should be cautious and focus on the specific attribute and not start discussing other attributes unless there are necessary links across. Some examples of questions you might be asked are these:

Question	What it is asking
Critically assess the philosophical problems raised by belief that God is omnipotent.	This question is asking you to identify all the problems that are raised by the notion of God's omnipotence. Primarily you should focus on the different interpretations of omnipotence and then discuss how it affects the way we read revelation. You might want to mention the problem of evil in this also.

Evaluate the claim that God is omnipotent	This question is asking for an evaluation of the classical attribute of omnipotence. Here you can discuss the classical scholarship as well as Greek ideas of God/the Prime Mover being all powerful.
Assess the claim that the universe shows no evidence of the existence of a benevolent God.	The clue in this question is 'evidence of benevolence'. The problem of evil is the obvious issue at hand as there is evident suffering; however, this is not a problem of evil question. Discuss the challenges to God's benevolence from the problem of evil, but also discuss the problem of miracles. In response, use morality and the theodicies.
Critically assess the philosophical problems raised by believing in an omnibenevolent God.	The problems of believing in a benevolent God are the problem of evil, the problem of miracles, hell and morality. Discuss these problems and then evaluate the extent to which they can be resolved.

Exercise: Analyse this question: 'The classical attributes of God are untenable.' Discuss.

Essay Skills – Linking Back to the Question

A line of reasoning needs to be evident throughout the essay, from the thesis statement all the way through to the conclusion. This can be done through use of links back to the question. At the end of every paragraph ask yourself: "have I answered the question?" This does not mean that every paragraph needs to state your thesis statement. This cannot be the case as you need to challenge it and give alternate views. However, it does mean that at the end of every paragraph you need to make sure that you have either defended your thesis statement, or made a challenge against it that brings it into question.

Ways you can link back to the main thesis, are these:

Therefore, it can be seen that God cannot be understood to be benevolent since…

This brings into question God's omnipotence as an all-powerful God would…

This supports the belief that God must be all-loving as…

This challenges the argument that God can do the illogical as well as logical as…

Exercise: Write a paragraph supporting and challenging the exercise 1 exam question. At the end of each paragraph write a link back to the question ensuring that you make it clear whether the paragraph supports or challenges your thesis statement.

God's Omniscience

Structure of Thought

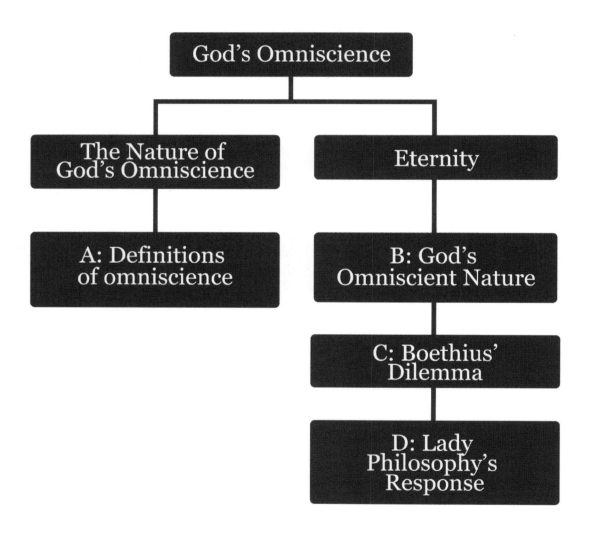

Omniscience

A. Definitions of Omniscience

Limited Knowledge

Omniscience is the belief that God has all knowledge. This has been defined in various ways. One understanding is that God has all knowledge that is logically possible for a being to have within a spatio-temporal universe, that is, knowledge of the present and the past. In Richard Swinburne's Is there a God?, he notes that God must be present in time in order to know what is happening in time.

For myself I cannot make much sense of this [all events being simultaneously present to God] suggestion – for many reasons, For example, I cannot see that anything can be meant by saying that God knows (as they happen) the events of AD 1995 unless it means that he exists in 1995 and knows in 1995 what is happening then...hence I prefer that understanding of God being eternal as his being everlasting rather than as his being timeless. (Richard Swinburne)

Exercise: What does it mean for God to have limited knowledge?

What conclusion is Swinburne making about the nature of God's eternity?

Unlimited Knowledge

St Thomas Aquinas, in Summa Theologica, comments that since God is not physical, and knowledge is not physical, God can possess knowledge. Aquinas, stemming from his Aristotelian influences, argues that God is outside of space and time and so can know past present and future.

God has knowledge because knowledge is not physical. Though humans gain knowledge through experience using their physical bodies, the knowledge itself is not physical. In this way, the non-physical God can possess knowledge. (Thomas Aquinas)

Exercise: What is the difference between limited and unlimited interpretation of God's omniscience?

Compare Swinburne's and Aquinas' approach to how God can possess knowledge.

Alternate Ways of Interpreting God's Knowledge

Friedrich Schleiermacher attempted to define God's knowledge as a form of intimate knowledge of friendship rather than an absolute knowledge.

God's omniscience is like the knowledge that close friends have of each other's behaviour, intimate but not controlling.

Louis of Molina suggested that God's omniscience might include all possible outcomes of the future. Elizabeth Anscombe responded to Molina's interpretation suggesting that it made no sense to speak of possible outcomes.

There was no such thing as how someone would have spent his life if he had not died as a child.

Exercise: How might Schleiermacher's interpretation respond to the problem of evil and suffering?

In what way does this interpretation free God from accountability for human suffering?

Interpreting Scriptural Accounts of God's Omniscience

God's omniscience is suggested in various places in the Bible. In some books it appears as though God learns as humans act, similar to Swinburne's limited interpretation. In other places, God appears to have eternal knowledge, similar to Aquinas' interpretation.

Uriah's wife heard that her husband was dead. David had her brought to his house. She became his wife. But the LORD was not pleased with what David had done. (2 Samuel 11: 26f)

Can you bind the chains of Pleiades, or loose the cords of Orion? Can you lead forth the Mazzoroth in their season, or can you guide the Bear with its children? Do you know the ordinances of the heavens? Can you establish their rule on the earth? (Job 12, 38: 31ff)

Exercise: What does this passage suggest about how God knows of David's actions?

B. God's Omniscient Nature

God as Everlasting

Richard Swinburne's definition of God's omniscience requires that God's eternity be seen as everlasting within a spatio-temporal universe. That is, God exists within time. This also allows for God to be responsible for miracles and answering prayers as He can respond to human action and pleas.

Nicholas Wolterstorff, in God Everlasting, said that our desire for God to be outside of time comes from our constant feelings of regret over the past and evils that have occurred.

...The feeling, deep seated in much of human culture, that the flowing of events into the irrecoverable and unchangeable past is a matter of deep regret. Our bright actions and shining

moments do not long endure. The gnawing of time bites all. And out evil deeds can never be undone. They are forever to be regretted … regrets over the persuasive pattern of what transpires within time have led whole societies to place the divine outside of time – freed from the bondage of temporality. (Wolterstorff)

Exercise: Why would it make sense for God to be within time if we were to believe that God both answers prayers and performs miracles?

How might Wolterstorff's perspective affect the way we interpret the problem of evil and suffering and more specifically, attempts at theodicy?

God as Impassible

In Genesis we find indication that God is immanently in the world and responds to events in the world:

8 They heard the sound of the Lord God walking in the garden at the time of the evening breeze, and the man and his wife hid themselves from the presence of the Lord God among the trees of the garden. 9 But the Lord God called to the man, and said to him, "Where are you?" (Genesis 3:8-9)

In support of this, Nelson Pike argued that if God is to be seen as having any kind of relationships with human beings, then God could not be impassible (unchangeable):

Where there are relationships there must be a response to the feelings and needs of each. God is not impassible because he responds to our needs.

In response to this perspective, R. S. Franks suggested that in fact God must be distant and unchangeable ,as a fact of God's nature:

God's impassibility means he cannot be acted upon, not that he is emotionless. Compassion is part of God's nature. (R.S. Franks)

Plato discusses the Essential FORM of Goodness as the unchanging source of life:

God's eternity is apparent through the unchanging world of Forms. God is the first in the chain of cause-and-effect; he is not caused or affected.

Aristotle similarly describes the Prime Mover as pure actuality and as such unchangeable:

Since all things have causes there must have been an uncaused cause, a Prime Mover, an unchanged changer...God. The Prime Mover sets things in motion by is itself unaffected by any cause, God cannot be acted upon.

Exercise: How does Pike's interpretation of God's nature differ from St Thomas Aquinas' and Aristotle's interpretation?

Why might Franks insist that God must be seen as impassible?

Augustine on God as Timeless

In Exodus 3:14, God reveals his name as 'I AM that I AM', a similar revelation as Aristotle's understanding of God as pure actuality: being.

God said to Moses, "I AM who I AM. This is what you are to say to the Israelites: "I AM has sent me to you" (Exodus 3:14)

Augustine, in Confessions, argued that God must be outside of space and time as God is the creator of all things.

Therefore, since you are the maker of all times, if there was a time before you made heaven and earth, why do they say that you rested from work? You made that very time, and no times could pass by before you made those times. But if there was no time before heaven and earth, why do they ask what you did then? There was no "then," where there was no time. [God] surpasses all times [since he occupies] an ever present eternity. You have made all times, and you are before all times, and not at any time was there no time.(Confessions)

If there was no time before heaven and earth, why do they ask what you did then? There was no "then", where there was not time. God is unchangeable (impassible) and thus cannot lose or gain characteristics. God simply knows our choices, which are free will choices.

Exercise: How does this passage from Exodus support the Aristotelian notion of God being pure act, and Thomas Aquinas' notion of God being timeless?

Aquinas on God as Timeless

Aquinas, in Selected Writings on God's Eternity, stated that God's eternity is a simultaneous whole. In this way, God must be outside of space and time in order to perceive all of time as one whole.

Eternity is simultaneously whole, while time is not, eternity measuring abiding existence and time measuring change...the primary intrinsic difference of time and eternity is that eternity exists as a simultaneous whole and time does not. (Aquinas)

Anthony Kenny in The God of the Philosophers, challenged Aquinas' interpretation of eternity as a simultaneous whole, arguing that if all events were simultaneous with eternity, then all events would be happening at the same time.

If all time is simultaneously present to God the meaning of the world 'simultaneous' entails that all of time is happening at the same moment which appears to be incoherent. ... On St. Thomas Aquinas' view, my typing of this paper is simultaneous with the whole of eternity. Again, on this view, the great fire of Rome is simultaneous with the whole of eternity. Therefore, while I type these very words, Nero fiddles heartlessly on. (Anthony Kenny)

Paul Helm, in Eternal God: A Study of God without Time, responded to Kenny's criticism of Aquinas' notion of eternity and sought to further define what is meant by eternity.

God, considered timeless, cannot have temporal relations with any of his creation. He is timeless in this sense of being time free. This at once provides an answer to the reductio brought by philosophers such as Kenny and Swinburne by denying that what any of us is now doing is taking place at the same time as anything God is doing. (Paul Helm)

Exercise: To what extent does God need to be seen as timeless if we see Him as 'Creator'?

How does God's knowledge being simultaneously whole require that God's eternity is outside of space and time?

Prayer

In Summa Theologica, Aquinas states that God wills from eternity. That God's nature is eternal and transcendently apart from the rest of the universe.

Prayer is the act of being aware of God's activity in the world, either directly (primary agency) or through others (secondary agency) it is not about making requests. God's nature and existence are one and the same ... God's nature is love. God does not have a body which has characteristics, God is simply God; he is immaterial. God wills whatever he does form eternity. God cannot be changed by anything outside himself – he is impassible. Time and change are inseparable; since God cannot change, He cannot be in time. (Aquinas)

Fr Mike Schmitz from the YouTube channel Ascension Presents commented on prayer and stated that when we pray we 'do not change God' as God is impassible and eternal. Instead, human prayer is like a child helping their parents work. The parents do not need the child's help, but in helping it builds a relationship between the two.

Exercise: What is the problem of prayer if God is outside space and time?

How does Aquinas respond to the problem of prayer?

Eternity

A. Boethius' Dilemma

The Problem with Omniscience – Consolations of Philosophy Book V

If God's omniscience is unlimited (knowing past, present and future) and He exists eternally (outside of time and space) then there is a problem for human free will. If God knows our actions, then we are not free to act. This problem was taken up by Boethius in his conversation with Lady Philosophy in Consolations of Philosophy Book V.

If God foresees all things and cannot in anything be mistaken, that, which His Providence sees will happen, must result. Wherefore if it knows beforehand not only men's deeds but even their designs and wishes, there will be no freedom of judgement For there can neither be any deed done, nor wish formed, except such as the infallible Providence of God has foreseen. (Boethius)

Exercise: What does Boethius mean by Providence?

Draw this image. Label it as follows:

- The eye = God's Providence
- The left person = today
- The right person = tomorrow
- The vertical arrow = Providence seeing my actions today
- The diagonal arrow = Providence seeing my actions tomorrow

The Problem with Providence – Consolations of Philosophy Book V

If a man sits down, it must be that the opinion, which conjectures that he is sitting, is true; but conversely, if the opinion concerning the man is true because he is sitting, he must be sitting down. There is therefore necessity in both cases: the man must be sitting, and the opinion must be true. But he does not sit because the opinion is true, but rather the opinion is true because his sitting down has preceded it. Thus, though the cause of the truth of the opinion proceeds from the other fact, yet there is a common necessity on both parts.

Exercise: Copy this image. Label it as follows:

The stick person = The man is sitting.
The eye = It is the opinion that the man is sitting.

Explain how this shows mutual necessity.

The Problem with Free Will – Consolations of Philosophy Book V

Boethius goes on to explain how if Providence does see our future actions then not only are we not free to act, but there is no point in prayer and judgement.

In like manner we must reason of Providence and future events. For even though they are foreseen because they are about to happen, yet they do not happen because they are foreseen. None the less it is necessary that either what is about to happen should be foreseen of God, or that what has been foreseen should happen; and this alone is enough to destroy all free will.

In vain are rewards or punishments set before good or bad, for there is no free or voluntary action of the mind to deserve them and what we just now determined was most fair, will prove to be most unfair of all, namely to punish the dishonest or reward the honest, since their own will does not put them in the way of honesty or dishonesty, but the unfailing necessity of development constrains them. Wherefore neither virtues nor vices are anything, but there is rather an indiscriminate confusion of all deserts. And nothing could be more vicious than this; since the whole order of all comes from Providence, and nothing is left to human intention, it follows that our crimes, as well as our good deeds, must all be held due to the author of all good. (Boethius)

Exercise: Paragraph 1: How does the existence of necessity destroy free will according to Boethius?

Paragraph 2: What is Boethius' problem with God rewarding and punishing?

Consider when God discovered David's murder of Uriah in 1 Samuel (see above). How might a timeless and everlasting God be differently accountable?

B. Lady Philosophy's Response

The Nature of God's Knowledge – Consolations of Philosophy Book V

Boethius was consoled in his dilemma over free will by the voice of Philosophy appearing as Lady Philosophy in Consolations of Philosophy Book V. She outlines the problem and how we can resolve it through a change in our understanding of God's knowledge.

The cause of this obscurity is that the working of human reason cannot approach the directness of divine foreknowledge.

Every subject, that is known, is comprehended not according to its own force, but rather according to the nature of those who know it. The roundness of a body may be known in one way by sight, in another way by touch. A man himself is differently comprehended by the senses, by imagination, by reason, and by intelligence. Higher still is the view of the intelligence, which reaches above the sphere of the universal, and with the unsullied eye of the mind gazes upon that very form of the kind in its absolute simplicity. The higher power of understanding includes the lower, but the lower never rises to the higher. The true intelligence is God's alone. (Boethius)

Exercise: What is the obscurity?

What does Lady Philosophy mean by directness of divine foreknowledge?

The Nature of Eternity – Consolations of Philosophy Book V

Lady Philosophy goes on to explain how God's eternity works. This is very similar to Aquinas' presentation (written later), and shows eternity as a simultaneous possession of all of time at once.

God is eternal. Eternity is the simultaneous and complete possession of infinite life. All that lives under the conditions of time moves through the present from the past to the future; there is nothing set in time which can at one moment grasp the whole space of its lifetime. It cannot yet comprehend to-morrow; yesterday it has already lost. And in this life of to-day your life is no more than a changing, passing moment. For though it apprehends and grasps a space of infinite lifetime, it does not embrace the whole simultaneously; it has not yet experienced the future. What we should rightly call eternal is that which grasps and possesses wholly and simultaneously the fullness of unending life, which lacks naught of the future, and has lost naught of the fleeting past; and such an existence must be ever present in itself to control and aid itself, and also must keep present with itself the infinity of changing time. (Boethius)

Exercise: How does this extract from Consolations of Philosophy appear to have influenced Aquinas' view of God's eternity?

How does Providence see our "future" actions?

The Nature of Necessity – Consolations of Philosophy Book V

Lady Philosophy gives the example of the man walking and the sun rising and contrasts them. One is moving freely and the other by compulsion.

When you see at the same time a man walking on the earth and the sun rising in the heavens, you see each sight simultaneously, yet you distinguish between them, and decide that one is moving voluntarily, the other of necessity. In like manner the perception of God looks down upon all things without disturbing at all their nature, though they are present to Him but future under the conditions of time. God looks in His present upon those future things which come to pass through free will. Therefore if these things be looked at from the point of view of God's insight, they come to pass of necessity under the condition of divine knowledge; if, on the other hand, they are viewed by themselves, they do not lose the perfect freedom of their nature. (Boethius)

Exercise: What is the difference between what makes the sun rise and the man walk?

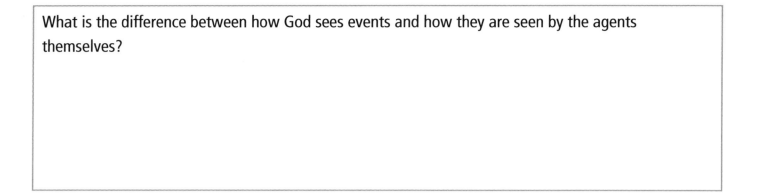

What is the difference between how God sees events and how they are seen by the agents themselves?

Judgement

The final part of Lady Philosophy's response deals with the fairness of God's judgement. Boethius complained that if we do not have free will God can neither reward nor punish. Lady Philosophy responds directly to that complaint.

Since all judgement apprehends the subjects of its thought according to its own nature, and God has a condition of ever-present eternity, His knowledge, which passes over every change of time, embracing infinite lengths of past and future, views in its own direct comprehension everything as though it were taking place in the present. Whence Providence is more rightly to be understood as a looking forth than a looking forward, because it is set far from low matters and looks forth upon all things as from a lofty mountain-top above all.

Thus, therefore, mortal men have their freedom of judgment intact. And since their wills are freed from all binding necessity, laws do not set rewards or punishments unjustly. God is ever the constant foreknowing overseer, and the ever-present eternity of His sight moves in harmony with the future nature of our actions, as it dispenses rewards to the good, and punishments to the bad. Hopes are not vainly put in God, nor prayers in vain offered: if these are right, they cannot but be answered. Turn therefore from vice: ensue virtue: raise your soul to upright hopes: send up on high your prayers from this earth. If you would be honest, great is the necessity enjoined upon your goodness, since all you do is done before the eyes of an all-seeing Judge. (Boethius)

Exercise: Paragraph 1: Why is God in a unique place to judge human beings?

Paragraph 2: What does Boethius mean by 'looking forth'?

Paragraph 3: How does Lady Philosophy respond to the problem of Free Will?

Paragraph 4: How does Lady Philosophy respond to the problem of reward and judgement?

Essay Skills

Types of Questions

Questions on this topic might focus on God's omniscience, God's eternity, the issue with rewards and punishments or free will. Whichever it asks, the arguments for God's eternity are central to all of it and this matter needs to be fully understood and used to respond to all questions on this topic. Some examples of questions you might be asked are these:

Question	What it is asking
Evaluate the philosophical problems raised by the belief that God is eternal.	The problems with God as eternal are: timeless vs everlasting and how an eternal God affects free will. If you have time, deal with rewards and punishments.

Critically assess the problems for believers who say that God is omniscient.	The problems with God's omniscience are: the issues of free will, the kind of omniscience God has – limited or unlimited – and the issue of rewards and punishments.
Boethius was successful in his argument that God rewards and punishes justly. Discuss.	You need to lay out Boethius' issues first and then respond to them. Make sure there is a clear response to rewards and punishments.
Evaluate the claim that God can fairly judge.	Here you need to lay out the need for God to be eternal in a timeless sense, compare that to an everlasting sense, and then deal with Boethius' dilemma and the resolution.

Exercise: Analyse this question: 'Evaluate the claim that God is eternal.' Discuss.

Essay Skills – Resolving Challenges

In your introduction you have told the reader what your perspective is and you throughout your essay you have laid out the arguments for and against. It is very important, as you go through your essay, 1. To be balanced and 2. To resolve all challenges. If you are not balanced it will look as though you are not evaluating properly enough. You must engage with the question and identify where your thesis statement runs into problems and explore those problems. However, you must resolve issues. If you do not, by the time the reader comes to your conclusion it will be a wonder why you have drawn that conclusion at all.

For example:

- Question: God cannot reward and punish fairly. Discuss
- Thesis statement: God can reward and punish fairly.
- Argument 1: God is eternal.
- Challenge 1: An eternal God means we do not have free will.
- Argument 2: God is timeless.
- Challenge 2: Providence is never wrong.
- Conclusion: God can reward fairly.

The problem here is that while argument 1 and 2 support the thesis statement, challenge 1 and 2 undermine it. This shows balance, yes, but the challenges are not resolved. If they are not resolved the thesis statement remains unjustified and any conclusion is invalid as it does not follow from the essay.

A better way of writing the essay would be:

- Questions: God cannot reward and punish fairly. Discuss
- Thesis statement: God can reward and punish fairly.
- Argument 1: God is eternal.
- Challenge 1: An eternal God means we do not have free will.
- Response 1: However, Augustine shows God's eternal nature allows free will.
- Argument 2: God is timeless.
- Challenge 2: Providence is never wrong.
- Response 2: Lady Philosophy shows that God sees eternally not effecting freedom.
- Conclusion: God can reward fairly.

This way, you are still keeping the essay balanced but also responding to any challenges so that the conclusion (your thesis statement) is the only logical conclusion.

Exercise: Write your own example of the above essay outline for the exercise 1 question.

Religious Language – Classical

Apophatic Way

Structure of Thought

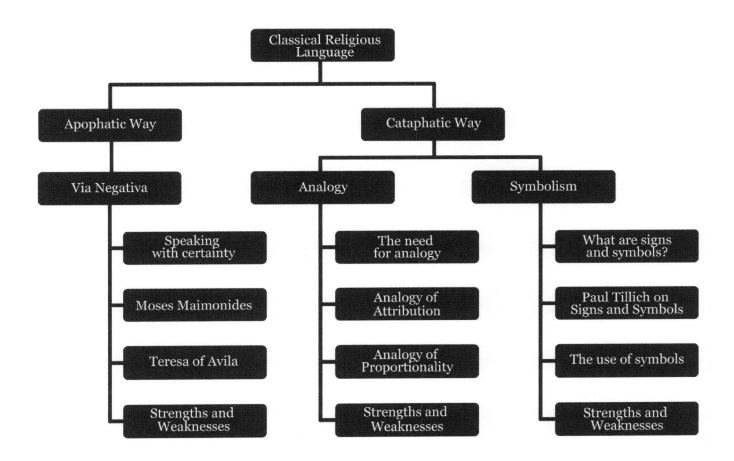

Via Negativa

A. Moses Maimonides

Understanding God through Negation

Moses Maimonides was the Jewish theologian who argued that any attempt to speak about God using positive language was ultimately futile as you could never say anything about God that was meaningful. Further, in Guide for the Perplexed, he argued that it was unnecessary to attempt to do so as you would be more likely to arrive at the notion of God through negation: Via Negativa.

There is no necessity at all for you to use positive attributes of God with the view of magnifying Him in your thought ... I will give you ... some illustrations, in order that you may better understand the propriety of forming as many negative attributes as possible, and the impropriety of ascribing to God any positive attributes. (Maimonides)

A person may know for certain that a 'ship' is in existence, but he may not know to what object that name is applied, whether to a substance or to an accident; a second person then learns that a ship is not an accident; a third, that it is not a mineral; a fourth, that it is not a plant growing in the earth; a fifth, that it is not a body whose parts are joined together by nature; a sixth, that it is not a flat object like boards or doors; a seventh, that it is not a sphere; an eight, that it is not pointed; a ninth, that it is not round shaped; nor equilateral; a tenth, that it is not a solid.

It is clear that this tenth person has arrived at the correct notion of a 'ship' by the foregoing negative attributes.

In this example, Moses Maimonides attempts to show that through the process of elimination, we can finally arrive at the notion of God having eliminated every other possibility. By the process of elimination we can arrive at the ship and in the same way we can arrive at the notion of God.

Exercise: What does Moses Maimonides mean when he says it is futile to speak positively about God?

The Danger of Positive Language

Moses Maimonides went on to argue that not only was it not necessary to speak positively about God, but to do so would ultimately result in a loss of faith. By this he was implying that the process by which we apply positive language is one of reducing God from the being of wonder to language born of human experience which is mundane.

In the same manner you will come nearer to the knowledge and comprehension of God by the negative attributes ... I do not merely declare that he who affirms attributes of God has not sufficient knowledge concerning the Creator ... but I say that he unconsciously loses his belief in God. (Maimonides)

Exercise: What does Moses Maimonides mean when he says that positive language will finally result in losing faith?

Consider Sigmund Freud and the notion that we project our desires externally to a 'god' figure outside of us. Now consider Moses Maimonides' argument that when we use positive language we reduce God to language of our own experiences. In what way does Moses Maimonides' challenge compare to Freud's idea that God is a neurosis.

Thought Point

In the Ethics specification, we encounter Freud's theory fo the subconscious mind in the section on Conscience. In The Future of an Illusion Freud considers religious belief to be an infantile projection of a father-figure onto God - and conscience itself is seen as a creation of childhood experiences of praise and blame.

Evaluating Moses Maimonides

Brian Davies argued that Moses Maimonides' example was unhelpful as a process of elimination never actually arrives at what a thing is. One needs to know what you are talking about in order to ever arrive at the final notion. I have experience of ships and so I might be able to understand the notion that Moses Maimonides intends, however, there is no reason why I would ever guess that is what he means.

Only saying what something "is not" gives no indication of what it actually is, and if one can only say what God is not, one cannot understand him at all. Suppose I say that there is something in my room, and suppose I reject every suggestion about what is in my room. Going back to the quotation from Maimonides ... it is simply unreasonable to say that someone who has all the negations mentioned in it 'has almost arrived at the correct notion of a "ship". He could equally well be thinking of a wardrobe. (Brian Davies)

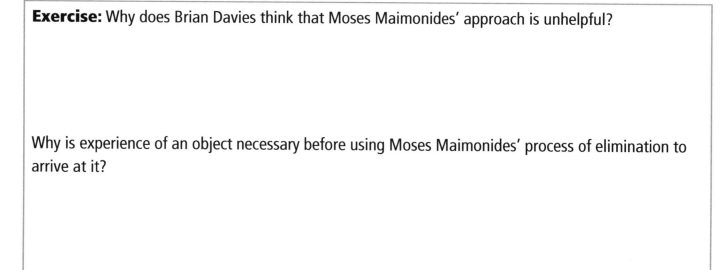

Exercise: Why does Brian Davies think that Moses Maimonides' approach is unhelpful?

Why is experience of an object necessary before using Moses Maimonides' process of elimination to arrive at it?

B. Teresa of Avila

Ineffable Experiences

Teresa of Avila was a Spanish nun who had mystical experiences which she recorded in her autobiography. While some of the experiences were describable, for example her ecstasy, some are ineffable and she articulates how she was unable to describe any aspect of them. In her autobiography she describes how she was unable to describe how she was certain about Christ's presence. This ineffable articulation is a form of Via Negativa.

I went at once to my confessor, to tell him about it. He asked me in what form I had seen Him. I told him that I had not seen Him at all. Then he asked me how I knew it was Christ. I told him that I did not know how, but that I could not help realising that He was beside me, and that I saw and felt this clearly. (St Teresa)

Exercise: Look through some examples of Teresa of Avila's experiences and separate the ineffable ones with the describable ones.

How were any of Teresa of Avila's experiences examples of Via Negativa?

Supporting the Via Negativa

Pseudo-Dionysius argued that it was impossible to make statements about God, such as 'God is good' as those terms have no meaning for God as they are human terms. This is an interesting way of responding to the problem of evil and suffering as the challenge against God's existence is based on a solid and agreed definition of benevolence and omnipotence. If we do not have a definition of those terms for God then that argument has no meaning. This also means that we can never make statements about God.

You cannot say that God is good because you do not know what it means to say that 'God is good'. (Pseudo-Dionysius)

Rudolph Otto was the scholar who coined the phrase 'numinous' meaning the 'wholly other' which inspires awe because of its mystery. He argued that religious language need not be positive as all it needed to do was to convey the mysterium tremendum et fascinans (fearful and fascinating mystery). If Via Negativa could do this, then that is all that is necessary. In fact, the very nature of Via Negativa places God outside our realm of understanding as it eliminates from God any terms that are based in human experience thus placing God as being 'wholly other'.

Exercise: What does Pseudo-Dionysius mean when he says we have no idea what it means to call God good?

How can we use this argument as an argument to defend God against the problem of evil?

Challenging the Via Negativa

In Summa Theologica St Thomas Aquinas argued that speaking about God was not simply a matter of negation but rather that there was a sense of learning about God and building a relationship. Positive language allows us to make statements about our relationship with God. It is not merely a means of making literal assertions. That would be impossible. It serves a purpose that is beyond literal.

When we say "God is alive" we mean more than "God is not mortally dead" In regard to what they express, these words apply literally to God. But as regards their manner of expressing it, they don't apply literally to God; for their manner of expression is appropriate only to creatures.
(Aquinas)

Exercise: What do we mean when we say God is alive?

In what way is language used to build relationships?

Cataphatic Way

Structure of Thought

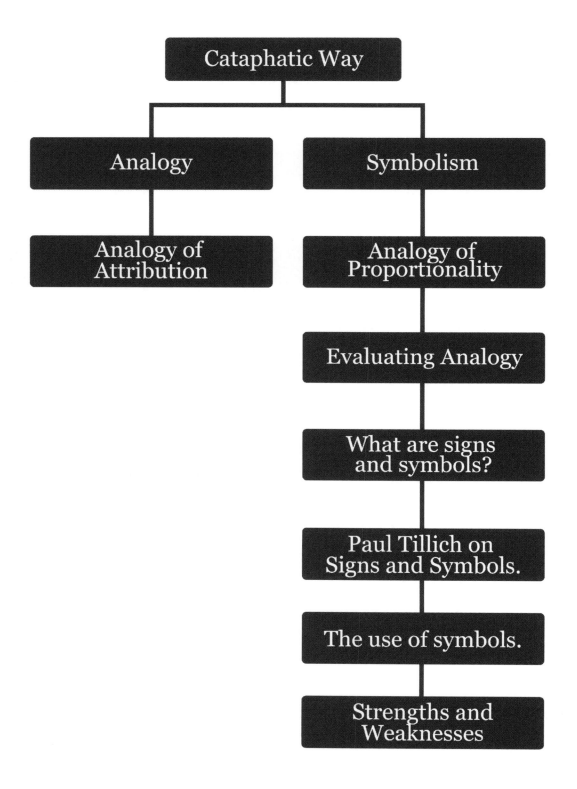

Analogy

A. Analogy of Attribution

Scriptural Use of Analogy

Analogy is a method of language that exists within scripture and has been long used as a means of talking about God. When God is compared to a potter and we as the clay, or God is the craftsman and the world is the work of His hands these are all analogies. They are ways we learn about God through some comparison or analogy of something that we know and have experienced.

"This is how you should pray, "Our Father who art in heaven, hallowed by thy name'." (Matthew 6:9-13)

In the Gospels, Jesus of Nazareth Himself tells us to call God Father and used that analogy to help us to build a relationship with Him. God cannot be a father in the literal sense as fathers are biological parents and God is not a physical/biological entity. However, the analogy is fitting in the sense that in the same way that fathers are part of our creation process and care for us and sustain us, God created us, cares for and sustains us.

Analogy, then, is the linguistic method of building an idea of one thing by comparing it to another which we know and have experienced. In this way, religious tradition uses it to help members build a relationship with God.

Exercise: What does analogy mean?

Find two more examples of analogy in the Bible.

Medicine and Urine

St Thomas Aquinas argued that we could use analogy to help us talk about God. The firsts form was analogy of attribution whereby we can learn about God through our knowledge of something else. Aquinas' example was the medicine and the urine. As medicine would affect a person's health and so indirectly affect their urine, we can know the success of the medicine by testing the urine. Thus the attributes of the one are indicators of the other.

In this way, we can know about God from His creation. The world is good and allows life to flourish, so God must be good and desire life in the world. We can link this to the ideas of Natural Theology, and design arguments such as William Paley's in the Knowledge of God section of the Christian Thought paper.

Exercise: Draw a picture of medicine and a vial of urine. Now label them indicating what properties might make them good.

Brian Davies

Brian Davies supported analogy of attribution giving his own example of the baker and the bread. We experience the bread as soft and tasty and by those characteristics we can know that the baker is skilled and competent. The attributes of one indicate the attributes of the other.

Exercise: Give your own example of the relationship between two things allowing you to extrapolate one from the other.

Links to Aristotle

We can see clear links with Aristotle as the relationship between the two, medicine and urine, God and creation is the relationship between efficient and final cause. In this way, Aquinas' analogy of attribution is based on the relationship between what we know of a subject (the final cause) and what we can extrapolate about the cause of that subject (efficient cause).

Exercise: What is the relationship between a sculpture and a statue?

How much could you learn about a sculpture from a statue?

Weakness of Analogy of Attribution

Stephen Evans argued that there was a limited amount we could ever know about God. It makes no sense saying we can know of God's attributes from things we experience in the world as God is not of this world.

Additionally, Nietzsche argued that the fact that the world was broken would indicate that God Himself was incompetent. We have the challenges of natural suffering and the problem of evil and suffering all over again if we attempt to discuss God through our experiences of the world.

Exercise: If God is not of this world, what can we learn about Him from the world?

John Stuart Mill complained about all the natural suffering in the world. What would this tell us about a creator God?

B. Analogy of Proportionality

Meaning of Proportionality

Analogy of Proportionality is the approach that everything can be described and known by its own degree using similar terms. I can describe many things as good but I do not mean the same thing by it, all things can be good to their own degree. A good dog fetches the ball, a good husband does not cheat on his wife. Both are good but their goodness is proportional to themselves.

Aquinas' analogy of proportionality means that we can use terms like justice, love, goodness, power etc. for God knowing that the proportion to which they apply is infinite compared to the justice, love, goodness and power of a human being. We can use the term as we know what it means but its application is different as the subject is God, not humans.

Exercise: What is proportionality?

How can we talk about God using proportionality?

Ian Ramsey

Ian Ramsey developed this idea discussing models and qualifiers. We can know various models through our human experience: charity, kindness, sustenance etc. but through revelation of God we come to know at God's qualifier is infinite. Thus experience gives us the model and revelation of God gives us the qualifier. So we can talk meaningfully about God as we have the language born of experience and we understand the application from revelation.

Exercise: What is a model and what is a qualifier?

Compare Ramey's understanding to Aquinas'.

Thought Point: Links to Aristotle

Typically, the analogy of proportionality is also linked to Aristotle. In the same way that everything has its purpose/telos, everything can be good insofar as it fulfils that telos. A dog's telos is different from a human being's. Therefore, so long as we know that the telos of God is different to our telos, we can speak meaningfully about God.

Exercise: What is the telos of: a flower, a bee, & a cup?

The Weakness of Analogy

David Hume said that we cannot use analogy to talk about things we do not know. His famous quote was that the world is more like a cabbage than a machine. By this he meant that we can learn nothing about God from the world.

William Blackstone argued that all analogy had to be translated into univocal language to ever make sense. When I am comparing two dogs, I am comparing their literal eyes and muscles, I am not talking about things in different contexts and to different degrees. In fact Hume commented that you could not compare the cardiovascular system to the capillary system as they are two different things.

Exercise: What is the limitation of analogy?

Give two examples of things that are often compared that should not be compared.

What does Blackstone mean when he says that all analogy must be converted back into univocal language?

Symbols

A. Paul Tillich on Symbols

Signs and Symbols

Paul Tillich distinguishes between signs and symbols by way of their application. Signs are arbitrarily chosen and can mean whatever the collective mind decides. Whereas symbols are have a kinship with that which they represent. In Dynamics of Faith, Tillich articulates that a symbol must participate in that which they represent. He argues that religious language must be symbolic as at its very nature there is a sense of kingship between the terms used and the events they represent.

A sign points to something by arbitrary convention, but a symbol] participates in that to which it points. Symbols are not arbitrarily instituted...but grow out of the individual or collective unconsciousness. [This] growing out of the unconscious [means they] unlock hidden elements of our soul [and] open up levels of reality which otherwise are closed to us. Whatever we say about that which concerns us ultimately [i.e. Religion] ...has a symbolic meaning. The language of faith is the language of symbols. (Tillich)

This can be compared to John MacQuarrie's use of signs and symbols. In Principles of Christian Theology, MacQuarrie said there were two types of symbol, conventional ones and intrinsic ones.

The Conventional symbol has no connection with what it symbolises other than the fact that people have arbitrarily agreed to let it stand for this particular symbolizandum. The intrinsic symbol, on the other hand, has in itself a kinship with what it symbolises. When we speak of 'Symbolic Language', we generally have a fairly definite kind of language in mind, a kind in which the words are not understood in their direct or proper reference but in which they, so to speak, bounce off that to which they properly refer so as to impinge at a distance on a more remote subject-matter, to which the speaker wishes to refer. (MacQuarrie)

Exercise: What is the difference between a sign and a symbol for Tillich?

159

What does Tillich mean when he says that symbols participate in that to which it points?

Compare Tillich's signs and symbols to MacQuarrie's conventional and intrinsic symbols.

God as the Ground of our Being

In Systemic Theology, Tillich argued that the very nature of God as being transcendent and the basis for all that exists means that any conventional language rooted in human experience is insufficient. Therefore, language must take on a different function in order to mean anything about God. In this way, language is purely symbolic and can only make sense to users who understand the symbols in their religious context.

There can be no doubt that any concrete assertion about God must be symbolic, for a concrete assertion is one which uses a segment of finite experience in order to say something about him. It transcends the content of this segment, although it also includes it. The finite segment of reality which becomes a vehicle of a concrete assertion about God is affirmed and negated at the same time. It becomes a symbol, for a symbolic expression is one whose proper meaning is negated by that to which it points. And yet it is also affirmed by it, and this affirmation gives the symbolic expression an adequate basis for pointing beyond itself. (Tillich)

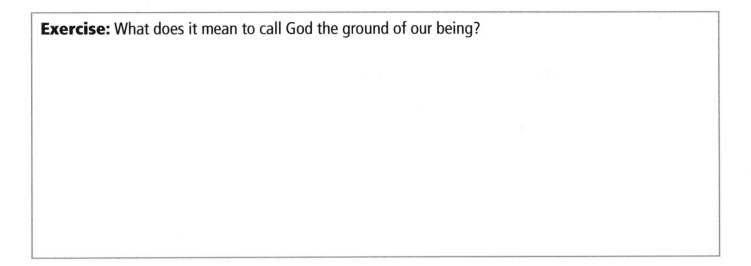

Exercise: What does it mean to call God the ground of our being?

B. The Need and Use of Symbols

Symbols in Scripture

Genesis 1 and 2 are deeply symbolic. Written post Babylonian Exile they carry stories and myths of the Babylonian people and reveal the ideas of God as shared by the Israelites. The idea of God creating in six days, the order in which things were created, e.g. light before sun etc. are all symbolic in that they represent ideas about God far beyond the literal meaning of the words.

Additionally, the Psalms are hymns about the glory and majesty of God which are not meant literally. They are reflections of a people in awe of the creator and are meant to be read as such. They are not historical or scientific but are reflecting and the language is like that of a love letter, not meant to be taken literally but rather to emphasise the relationship between the two parties.

John's Gospel is organised around seven great "signs' which are meant to have meanings deeper then the literal reading (for example when Jesus turns water into wine). These are:

- Changing water into wine at Cana in John 2:1-11 - "the first of the signs

- Healing the royal official's son in Capernaum in John 4:46-54.

- Healing the paralytic at Bethesda in John 5:1-15.

- Feeding the 5000 in John 6:5-14.

- Jesus walking on water in John 6:16-24.

Exercise: Give three examples of symbolic language in the Bible.

What does it mean to say that Genesis is true but not literal?

Historic Use of Symbols

Symbols were used by religious practitioners since the start of religion. Examples are of the ICTHUS within early Christianity, the Chi Rho, the idea of Christ as the Lamb of God and the cross itself. Each has a symbolic significance and goes beyond the sum of their literal component parts.

Exercise: What does ICTHUS mean? How is it a symbol of Christianity?

162

Symbols in Religious Tradition

Tillich used examples like atonement and baptism to show how language was ultimately symbolic. The act of atonement means little in literal terms but shared by users who understand the practice and feel represented by the symbolic meaning it represents, the term has life changing meaning.

The notion of baptism in literal terms is ridiculous. The thought of water washing away sin means nothing. However, within the Christian setting, carrying the beliefs about sin and the association to ritual cleansing, baptism means something far more significant and only has its meaning in symbolism. (Tillich)

Exercise: How essential are symbols for religious practice?

Is it true that all religious language is symbolic?

To what extent does analogy use symbolic language?

Limitations in the Use of Symbols

There are obvious limitations to the use of symbols. Some symbols change in meaning, e.g. the Swastika, other symbols lose their significance over time as cultures change, e.g. the ICTHUS becoming a bumper sticker etc.

It may be that religious language is symbolic as believers use it to participate in their faith, but it does not bridge the epistemic distance between God and Man. Calling God a shepherd may be a quaint symbol but it still does not tell us anything significant about God, only that shepherds in the past used their terms to label God.

Exercise: Give three examples of symbols that have lost their significance and meaning over time.

How does the fact that language has changed over time affect the usefulness of religious language as being symbolic?

To what extent is symbolic language more useful than Via Negativa, if at all?

Essay Skills

Types of Questions

Questions on this topic might focus on Via Negativa, Analogy or Symbolism or religious language as a whole. Question may ask for an analysis of one of the three types or may ask for an evaluation of one as the best or better than another. Depending on the nature of the question, candidates must be ready to evaluate the strengths and weaknesses of the type of language in question and if necessary make direct comparisons with other types. Some examples of questions you might be asked are these:

Question	What it is asking
You cannot talk positively about God.' Discuss.	You are being asked to analyse Via Negativa itself. There is no need to mention analogy or symbolism if you have enough to say without it.
To what extent does analogy tell us anything about God?	This is a question about analogy itself. Any link to Via Negativa or symbolism should be only to emphasise the usefulness of Analogy.
The only way to talk about God meaningful is through symbols.' Discuss.	This question is asking for a comparison as it specifically says 'the only way'. Since there are other ways – Via Negativa and Analogy, they should be used as comparisons.
Assess the claim that talking about God positively will ultimately result in a loss of faith.	This question is specifically referring to Moses Maimonides so he should be the main scholar. Since the question is asking about how positive language will lead to loss of faith, you can discuss analogy and symbolism as they are positive language. But be careful to keep the essay on track. It is not an analogy essay.

Exercise: Analyse this question: Assess the claim that you cannot talk about God without using Via Negativa.

Essay Skills – Writing Conclusions

The introduction and conclusion should, by themselves, tell the reader what the essay is about, what you think and why you think it. Where the introduction should lay out your plan and thesis statement, the conclusion should weigh up the main arguments you have signposted in the introduction and fully addressed in the essay proper. You need to leave 3-5 minutes for your conclusion otherwise it will look like a superficial sentence that does not serve a purpose.

Your conclusion has an important function: you need to show the reader that your thesis statement is justified. You need to use the conclusion to show that you have considered the different perspectives and resolved all the challenges. This is so important as if you do not resolve the challenges in the essay proper, you cannot justifiably draw your conclusion.

Your conclusion should include three things:

1.   A summary of the House's position.

2.   A summary of the Opposition.

3.   A reiteration of your thesis statement and why this is the correct position.

Most importantly, there should be nothing new in the conclusion.

When summarising the House or the Opposition it is important that you are not re-writing anything you have said. You are merely picking out the main scholar that represents that position and one or two important things they said and why they so well represent and defend that position.

A bad example of a sentence in the conclusion might be this: 'In conclusion, Tillich says that symbols are really important but some people disagree.' This tells us nothing about Tillich's position or why some might disagree. It is not a summary, it is a skimming over the point.

Another bad example of a sentence in the conclusion would be: 'In conclusion, Paul Tillich argued that God is the ground of our being, therefore, all language must be symbolic as it is only through symbols we can really bridge the gap between our language and God's nature; in the same way that we use the ICTHUS to understand about the nature of Jesus Christ, we use symbols in order to better understand God's nature and so build a positive relationship with Him.' This is far too detailed. This kind of analysis should be in the essay proper and not the conclusion.

A better sentence would be this: 'In conclusion, Tillich argues that all language is symbolic as it represents another idea and since we cannot know God directly, we can only use symbols to point to a transcendent idea.' This is detailed and simply. It encapsulates the point of Tillich's argument without going over the top. Follow this up with a sentence for the opposition and then defend your thesis statement.

Exercise: Write a conclusion for the essay title in exercise 1. Remember the three sentences.

Religious Language – 20th Century

Logical Positivism

Structure of Thought

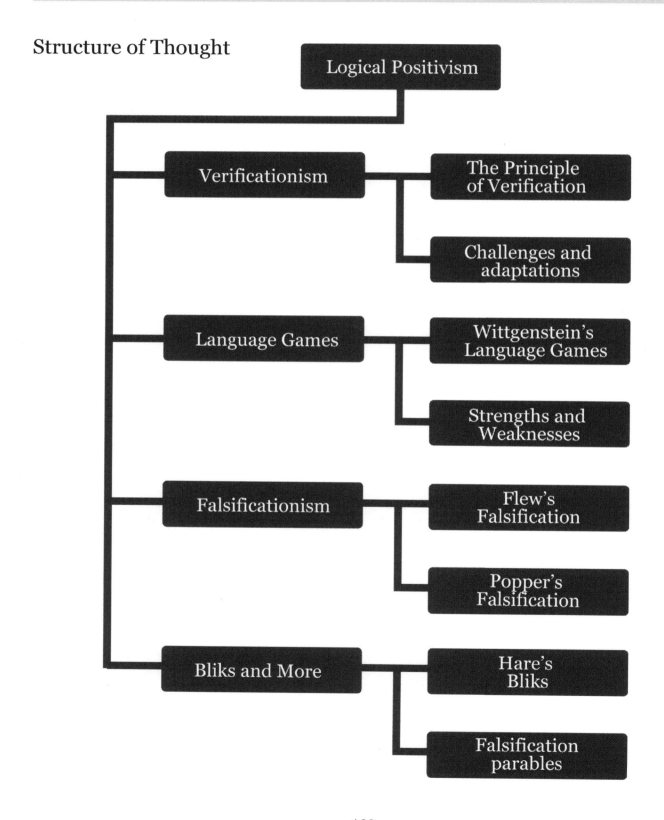

Logical Positivism

- Verificationism
  - The Principle of Verification
  - Challenges and adaptations
- Language Games
  - Wittgenstein's Language Games
  - Strengths and Weaknesses
- Falsificationism
  - Flew's Falsification
  - Popper's Falsification
- Bliks and More
  - Hare's Bliks
  - Falsification parables

Verificationism

A. The Principle of Verification

Moritz Schlick

Moritz Schlik's logical positivist position attempted to show that the only meaningful statements were those which could be sense-observed or which were tautologies. This is comparable to David Hume's postulation that there were only two fields of human study: relations of ideas (analytic propositions) and matters of fact (synthetic propositions).

If you cannot demonstrate with sense-observation how a statement is true then it is factually meaningless. (Schlick)

Exercise: Define analytic and synthetic propositions.

Give an example of an analytic and synthetic proposition.

A.J. Ayer

A.J. Ayer took on the position of the logical positivist which was called verificationism. This term means that the only meaningful statements are those which can be verified. Ultimately, the logical positivist movement was attempting to show that god-talk – any statements about or pertaining to God – was meaningless. Ayer further wanted to show that ethical statements were also nothing more than emotive statements.

There never comes a point where a theory can be said to be true. The most that one can claim for any theory is that it has shared the successes of all its rivals and that it has passed at least one test which they have failed"

Exercise: What does it mean to verify something?

To what extent does meaningfulness depend on verification?

B. Challenges and Adaptations

Richard Swinburne's Ravens

In God Talk is Evidently Not Meaningless, Richard Swinburne borrowed Carl Hemple's ravens example to show how we cannot always rely on the principle of verification when we discuss matters that are taken to be meaningful. To verify the statement: 'ravens are black', one would need to sense-observe every raven in existence. This is obviously ridiculous, but the statement does still have meaning.

People generally accept that Ravens are black, however, the statement 'are (at all times) black' cannot be verified, and as such it becomes meaningless. There are many areas of debate where the problem would be settling between people what was "admissible evidence" to decide the matter. Matters that are logically unverifiable are still matters of meaning and importance.

Strong and Weak Verification

In response to this ravens challenge, Ayer distinguished between strong and weak forms of verification, verification at the time of verifying and verification that can be done inductively using past experience and probability. Indeed, Ayer argued that the weak form was the most useful as even statements such as 'I am mortal' would be impossible to verify without killing myself.

My "strong" sense of the term "verifiable" had no possible application, and in that case there was no need for me to qualify the other sense of "verification" as weak; for on my own showing it was the only sense in which any proposition could conceivably be verified.(Ayer)

My mobile phone makes phone calls
Water boils at 100 degrees,
You can't breathe under water,
Humans cannot fly

Challenge of Theoretical Science

Ayer's requalification continued to run into problems. There are many statements which cannot be verified even in the weak sense which are still meaningful areas of study. At the time of the Logical Positivist movement it was impossible to make any statements about the dark side of the moon as no-one had ever seen it. Similarly, we could not make any meaningful statements about atoms and particles as we could not experience them and had no experience to make judgements.

Exercise: What is the problem with weak verification?

Identify one statement which are meaningful but cannot be verified using strong or weak verification.

Verification in Practice and Principle

In response to this challenge, Ayer recalculated the principle of verification as distinguishing between verification in practice (what we can verify in the strong sense) verification in principle (what we could in principle verify if we had the means).

Exercise: How is verification in practice similar to strong verification?

What kinds of meaningful scientific statements can never be verified using strong or weak verification?

John Hick's Challenge

John Hick used Ayer's requalification to argue that in fact god-talk was meaningful on the basis that it was verifiable in principle, perhaps not now but eschatologically – after death. He used his parable of the celestial city to demonstrate this.

Two men are travelling together along a road. One of them believes that it leads to the Celestial City, the other that it leads nowhere. But since this is the only road there is, both must travel it. Neither has been this way before, therefore neither is able to say what they will find around each corner. During their journey they meet with moments of refreshment and delight, and with moments of hardship and danger. All the time one of them thinks of his journey as a pilgrimage to the Celestial City … The other, however, believes none of this, and sees their journey as an unavoidable and aimless ramble … Yet, when they turn the last corner, it will be apparent that one of them has been right all the time and the other wrong. (John Hick)

Exercise: What is eschatological verification?

How does Hick use Ayer's principle of verification in principle to show that god-talk is meaningful?

Ayer's Second Version

Ayer requalified the verification principle once more by distinguishing between direct and indirect verification. This second version was based on evidence. If there is evidence that can be used to demonstrate a statement directly, then it was verifiable, much like strong and practical verification. If there was evidence that demonstrate a statement indirectly, then it was meaningful also.

A statement is directly verifiable if it is itself an observation-statement, or is such that in conjunction with one or more observation-statements it entails at least one observation-statement.

A statement is indirectly verifiable if, in conjunction with certain other premises it entails one or more directly verifiable statements which are not deducible from these other premises alone. (Ayer)

Exercise: Draw a table with two columns and title one column 'Is Verified' and the other column titled 'Can be Verified'. In the first column, summarise: the principle of verification, strong verification, verification in practice and direct verification. In the second column, summarise: weak verification, verification in principle and indirect verification.

Weaknesses of the Principle of Verification

Richard Swinburne maintained that even after the second version, the principle of verification excluded too much talk which was meaningful. He have the example of the toys in the cupboard that come to life when no-one is around. Which this cannot be verified, it is a perfectly meaningful thought experiment. Similarly, art, music and even history cannot be verified but are meaningful areas of discussion.

Finally, the principle of verification is itself meaningless as the statement: 'the only statements which are meaningful are sense-observations and tautologies' is itself not sense-observable nor a tautology.

Exercise: Why is the principle of verification ultimately not helpful when make statements of meaning?

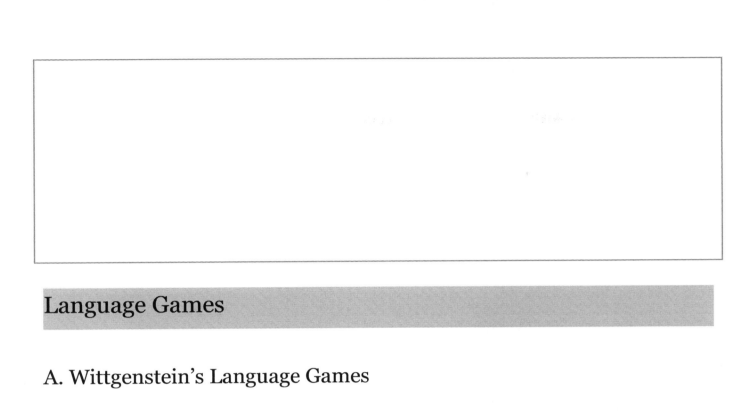

Language Games

A. Wittgenstein's Language Games

Language Games

Ludwig Wittgenstein started he career as a logical positivist and at the beginning of Tractatus stated: 'Whereof one cannot speak, thereof one must be silent.' However, in his work Philosophical Investigations, he changed his attitude to religious language and argued that all philosophical problems were linguistic ones.

He posited that all kinds of languages were different games with rules and uses and that one could not use one type of language in a setting where it did not apply. In the same way that the off-side rule and a red card are meaningless in chess but meaningful in football, in the same way religious language means nothing within science but is meaningful in theology.

Exercise: What is meant by the statement: 'Whereof one cannot speak, thereof one must be silent.'

What is a language game?

The Builders Example

Wittgenstein gave the example of the builders and the language they use and how they use it to be understood by each other.

Let us imagine a language ...The language is meant to serve for communication between a builder A and an assistant B. A is building with building-stones; there are blocks, pillars, slabs and beams. B has to pass the stones, and that in the order in which A needs them. For this purpose they use a language consisting of the words 'block', 'pillar', 'slab', 'beam'. A calls them out; --B brings the stone which he has learnt to bring at such-and-such a call. -- Conceive of this as a complete primitive language. (Wittgenstein)

Exercise: What is language to a builder?

What does it mean when a builder states: pillar, or beam?

What does Wittgenstein mean when he calls a builder's set of terms a primitive language?

Language as a Form of Life

Wittgenstein stated that a person's language was an essential part of their form of life. Language makes up what and how a person thinks. Therefore, we cannot state that any language is meaningless if it has meaning in its context and to its users.

23. The term 'language game' is meant to bring into prominence the fact that the 'speaking' of language is part of an activity, or form of life.

31. For a large class of cases—though not for all—in which we employ the word 'meaning' it can be defined thus: the meaning of a word is its use in the language.

Exercise: What does Wittgenstein mean when he calls language a s part of a form of life?

What does Wittgenstein mean when he says the meaning of a word is its 'use in language'?

B. Challenges and Uses

Norman Malcolm's Rational Justification

Norman Malcolm supported Wittgenstein's language games emphasising how it is unjust how theological beliefs need to be rationally justified in order for them to have any meaning.

The obsessive concern with the proofs of the existence of God reveals the assumption that in order for religious belief to be intellectually respectable it ought to have a rational justification. That is the misunderstanding. It is like the idea that we are not justified in relying on memory until memory has been proved reliable. (Norman Malcolm)

Exercise: Why is it unfair to expect rational justification for religious beliefs?

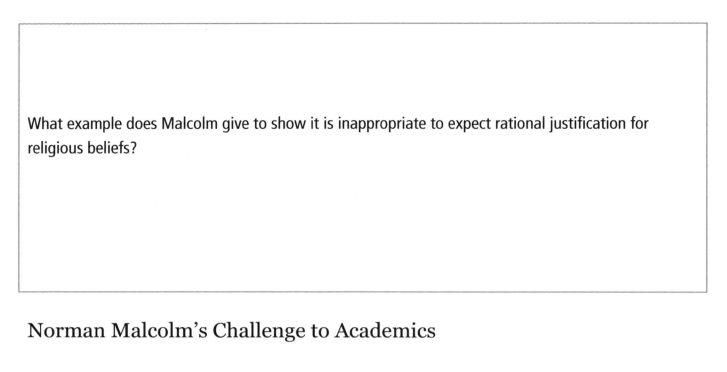

What example does Malcolm give to show it is inappropriate to expect rational justification for religious beliefs?

Norman Malcolm's Challenge to Academics

Malcolm argued that there was as sense of prejudice when it came to theological study that scientific statements were taken as being self-evident whereas religious ones were not. He commented that to the scientist, religion is an 'alien form of life'.

resent-day academic philosophers are far more prone to challenge the credentials of religion than of science, probably for a number of reasons. One may be the illusion that science can justify its own framework. Another may be that, by and large, religion is to university people an alien form or life. They do not participate in it and do not understand what it is all about. (Malcolm)

Thought-point: Alister McGrath's recent books concern the reinvigoration of natural theology as a holistic discipline which helps make sense of all reality. McGrath argues that empiricism led us to false concept of a Deist (prime mover, first cause) god whereas Christianity follows a God who is immanent as well as transcendent and by his Holy Spirit God informs and leads our thinking. It is reasonable in a post-modern understanding of 'reason' to believe in God.

Exercise: What is the problem with scientists expecting religious claims to be rationalised?

William Alston claimed that it was epistemic imperialism for scientists to question the authority of religious claims but not expect the same justification for scientific claims. How is this similar to Malcolm's point?

The Problem with Context

One challenge of language games is that it seeks to compartmentalise all forms of language as separate things and treat it as though they have nothing to do with each other. However, this is not always the case as some religious claims do seek to have a scientific basis, e.g. the resurrection of Christ is not seen as a purely 'religious' statement but as a real historical and scientific event.

Exercise: What is the problem with compartmentalising languages?

Explain how contextualising everything is a strength or weakness.

Falsification

Structure of Thought

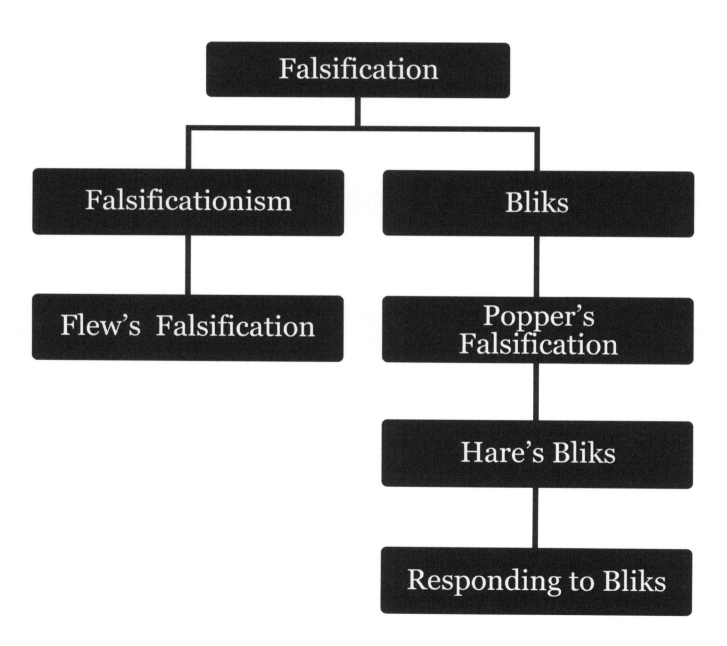

Falsificationism

A. Flew's Principle of Falsification

Unfalsifiability

The notion of falsifiability means accepting the theoretical conditions by which a statement or proposition might be refuted. If I were to say 'this pen is black' I am unconsciously stating: 'this pen is not green or blue or any other colour'. If it could be shown that the pen is red then my original claim is false. If I refuse to accept any condition by which my statement might be false, then my statement is unfalsifiable.

In Reason and Responsibility, Antony Flew argued that god-talk was meaningless as it was unfalsifiable.

For if the utterance is indeed an assertion, it will necessarily be equivalent to a denial of the negation of the assertion. And anything which would count against the assertion, or which would induce the speaker to withdraw it and to admit that it had been mistaken, must be part of (or the whole of) the meaning of the negation of that assertion. And to know the meaning of the negation of an assertion, is as near as makes no matter, to know the meaning of that assertion. And if there is nothing which a putative assertion denies then there is nothing which it asserts either: and so it is not really an assertion. (Flew)

Exercise: Define falsification and unfalsifiability.

When might a statement be seen as unfalsifiable?

The Parable of the Two Explorers

Flew borrowed John Wisdom's parable of the invisible gardener to make his point about unfalsifiability.

Once upon a time two explorers came upon a clearing in the jungle. In the clearing were growing many flowers and many weeds. One explorer says, 'Some gardener must tend this plot.' The other disagrees, 'There is no gardener.' So they pitch their tents and set a watch. No gardener is ever seen. 'But perhaps he is an invisible gardener.' So they set up a barbed-wire fence. They electrify it. They patrol with bloodhounds... But no shrieks ever suggest that some intruder has received a shock. No movements of the wire ever betray an invisible climber. The bloodhounds never give cry. Yet still the Believer is not convinced. 'But there is a gardener, invisible, intangible, insensitive to electric shocks, a gardener who has no scent and makes no sound, a gardener who comes secretly to look after the garden which he loves.' At last the Sceptic despairs, 'but what remains of your original assertion? Just how does what you call an invisible, intangible, eternally elusive gardener differ from an imaginary gardener or even from no gardener at all?' (Flew)

Exercise: If the believer in the gardener as the Christian and the sceptic as the atheist, summarise their different theological positions.

Death by a Thousand Qualifications

Flew went on to argue that the believer's statement was so eroded by qualification that it was no longer a statement at all. Thus, it was unfalsifiable. He argued that any theological statement, e.g. 'God loves me', 'God has a plan for us all' etc. were equally unfalsifiable as there is no condition under which the believer would accept that statement to be false.

If relentlessly pursued, the theologian will have to resort to avoiding action of qualification. And there lies that death by a thousand qualifications, which would, I agree, constitute a failure in faith as well as in logic. Christians make 'assertions' about the universe. Assertions are claims such as 'God made humans distinct from other species.' ...Therefore, God-Talk is meaningless as it is unfalsifiable.(Flew)

Exercise: What does Flew mean by 'eroded by qualification'?

Use the term 'death by a thousand qualifications' in a statement against god-talk.

B. Popper's Principle of Falsification

Karl Popper

Karl Popper was familiar with but never a part of the logical positivist movement. He was concerned with distinguishing between actual science and pseudo-science which was becoming culturally popular, e.g. astronomy and psychology which was pretending to be real science but which was not.

Popper argued, in Conjectures and Refutations, that such pseudo-science would destroy any attempt to prove them false by evading the process of falsification.

Astrologers were greatly impressed, and mislead, by what they believed to be confirming evidence – so much so that they were quite unimpressed by any unfavourable evidence … In order to escape falsification they destroyed the testability of their theory It was the problem of drawing a line between statements, or systems of statements, of the empirical sciences, and all other statements – whether they are of a religious or of a metaphysical character, or simply pseudo-scientific. Years later … I called this first problem of mine the "problem of demarcation". (Popper)

Exercise: What is pseudo-science?

What does it mean to say pseudo-scientists would destroy the testability of their theory?

Demarcation

Popper was not concerned with what was considering itself to be seen as 'meaningful', but with what was considering itself to be 'scientific'. He used the principle of falsification to demarcate between what was science and what was not.

The criterion of falsifiability is a solution to this problem of demarcation, for it says that statements or systems of statements, in order to be ranked as scientific, must be capable of conflicting with possible, or conceivable, observations … Falsification is demarcating (setting apart) scientific statements from other kinds of statements. The criterion of the scientific status of a theory is its falsifiability, or refutability, or testability.

Exercise: Which of these statements are scientific?

I am a human,
Jesus was the son of God,
When Jupiter moves through Pisces I will find my fortune,
All men have sexual desires for their mothers,

ii) How does Popper's approach to falsification show that Flew's use is itself a poor use of challenging God-talk? (Think about what Popper postulated that falsification demarcates).

Bliks

A. Hare's Bliks

A Blik

R.M. Hare sought to redeem the use of God talk by showing that religious claims were Bliks, unfalsifiable statements which had meaning and value to the claimants and impacted on their lives, thus making them meaningful.

Unfalsifiable statements can be meaningful to the claimant. If an unfalsifiable statement affects the way a person lives and interacts with people, then that statement is not simply meaningless, it has meaning to him/her. It can be called a Blik. A Blik is a claim about the world that is not falsifiable nor can it be tested. Bliks are ways of seeing the world and the difference between different people's bliks cannot be solved by observation of what the world is like. Conflicting bliks cannot be settled through rationale, reason or experience. Flew makes a mistake by treating religious statements as though they are scientific explanations.(Hare)

Exercise: What is a blik?

Why does it not matter if a blik is unfalsifiable?

Lunatic and the Dons

Hare gave the parable of the lunatic and the dons to emphasise how a blik can impact on a person's life. A Don is a lecturer at a University.

A certain lunatic is convinced that all dons want to murder him. His friends introduce him to all the mildest and most respectable dons that they can find, and after each of them has retired, they say, 'You see, he doesn't really want to murder you; he spoke to you in a most cordial manner; surely you are convinced now?' But the lunatic replies, 'Yes, but that was only his diabolical cunning; he's really plotting against me the whole time, like the rest of them; I know it I tell you'. However many kindly dons are produced, the reaction is still the same.(Hare)

Exercise: What is the lunatic's blik?

How does that blik affect his life?

What effect does the lunatic's friends' opinions have on the lunatic's blik?

Really Believing Something

In Theology Symposium on Theology and Falsification, Hare makes a point about why it matters when you really believe something and how that can affect your life.

When I am driving my car, it sometimes occurs to me to wonder whether my movements of the steering-wheel will always continue to be followed by corresponding alterations in the direction of the car. I have never had a steering failure, though I have had skids, which must be similar. Moreover, I know enough about how the steering of my car is made, to know the sort of thing that would have to go wrong for the steering to fail - steel joints would have to part, or steel rods break, or something - but how do I know that this won't happen? The truth is, I don't know; I just have a blik about steel and its properties, so that normally I trust the steering of my car; but I find it not at all difficult to imagine what it would be like to lose this blik and acquire the opposite one. People would say I was silly about steel; but there would be no mistaking the reality of the difference between our respective bliks - for example, I should never go in a motor-car . Yet I should hesitate to say that the difference between us was the difference between contradictory assertions. No amount of safe arrivals or bench-tests will remove my blik and restore the normal one; for my blik is compatible with any finite number of such tests.(Hare)

Exercise: Hare was under no illusion that the lunatic student was in fact a lunatic, however, what is the effect of a blik?

Hare's blik is that his car steering rods work. How might he act differently if he believed the opposite?

B. Responding to Bliks

John Wisdom

John Wisdom originally wrote the parable of the explorers to show how different people can see the same thing in very different ways. He also wanted to show that theological claims were not of the same type as scientific ones.

The nature of God is totally outside of our traditional methods of scientific enquiry – as a result is God-Talk meaningless?

Exercise: How does Wisdom support Norman Malcolm?

How does Wisdom support Hare?

Parable of the Partisan and the Stranger

Basil Mitchell presented this parable to show that sometimes believers make claims and do not allow any experience or evidence to gainsay them. This can be dangerous and he warned against it.

During the time of a war a Partisan meets a stranger claiming to be the leader of the resistance. The stranger urges the Partisan to have faith in him, even if he is seen to be acting against Partisan interests. The Partisan is committed to a belief in the stranger's integrity, but his friends think he is a fool to do so. The original encounter with the stranger gives the Partisan sufficient confidence to hold onto his faith in him even when there is evidence to the contrary. (Mitchell)

Theists do not accept evidence that counts against their beliefs Believers have to take care that religious beliefs are not just 'vacuous formulae to which experience makes no difference and which makes no difference to life.'

Exercise: What claim did the partisan have?

What made the partisan's claim unfalsifiable?

Flew against Bliks

Antony Flew responded to the use of bliks by arguing that many Christians do not make their assertions as bliks but as scientific statements.

Christians do not claim that this is a blik, but that it is a falsifiable claim. Believers will allow nothing to falsify their belief claims. Therefore, God-Talk is meaningless as it is unfalsifiable. Now it seems to people who are not religious as if there was no conceivable event or series of events the occurrence of which would be admitted by sophisticated religious people to be a sufficient reason for conceding "There wasn't a God at all". (Flew)

Exercise: How does Flew's argument compare to the argument against language games?

How does this argument align Flew's use of falsification with Popper's?

Essay Skills

Types of Questions

Questions on this topic might focus on verification or falsification. The two are generally exclusive and the examiners will not be expecting you to mention falsification in a question on meaningfulness which is a verification topic. However, given Flew's insistence that god-talk is unfalsifiable and so meaningless, there is a case for a crossover. However, this should not be the basis of your essays. Treat them as distinct. Some examples of questions you might be asked are these:

Question	What it is asking
God talk is meaningless.' Discuss.	This is a verificationism question. You should present the logical positivist variations of the verification principle and then use Swinburne and Hick to challenge them. Language Games should be used to respond to the principle of verification.
Assess the claim that language games adequately proves that god-talk is meaningful.	In this question, lead with a brief overview of the logical positivist position before delving into Language Games. Use Malcolm and even Wisdom to support Wittgenstein's position.
Falsification does not challenge religious belief.' Discuss.	This question expects you to explain Flew's version of falsification and then compare it with Popper's. Respond to this position with Hare and Wisdom.
To what extent do bliks make god-talk meaningful?	In this question, briefly overview Flew's position and then explain Hare's bliks, and the various other parables that explore god-talk, i.e. the partisan and the explorers.

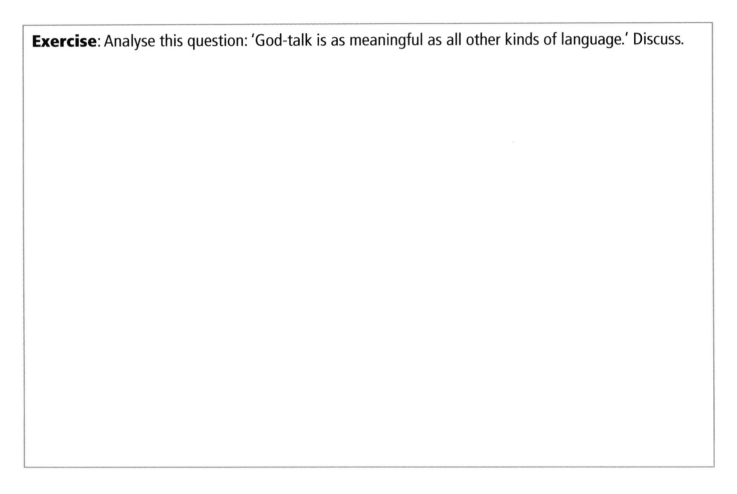

Exercise: Analyse this question: 'God-talk is as meaningful as all other kinds of language.' Discuss.

Essay Skills – Preparing for Any Essay

When you open your exam paper, you should not be surprised by anything you see. Any possible question should already be covered by an outline in your head. You do not have time to start planning your essay from scratch and in any syllabus area there are a limited number of underlying issues which you will be examined on. identify these and then prepare your line on them. With only 40 minutes per question you need to be ready for any question that is asked - but questions will be set within a range given by clues in the specification. All you need to do is decide which ones you are most confident with. In order to be at this level of confidence you need to prepare for any essay question that might come up by writing detailed essay plans and practicing various essay questions.

As an experiment, a colleague divided a class into two, those who had to practice throwing a ball of paper into the bin 1 meter away and those who had to practice throwing the ball of paper 50 cm and 1.5 meters away. When asked to throw a ball of paper 1 meter away, the second group performed better because they had practiced a variety of skills.

Use the skills demonstrated here in this pack to compile a bank of essay plans on various different questions focussing on general and specific aspects of the different topics. Read over them and rewrite them. Write the essays and then rewrite them.

Exercise: Write an essay plan for the question in the previous exercise.

About the Author

Andrew Capone is the Head of RE at St Simon Stock Catholic School, Maidstone. He has a Masters of Arts in Classical History and a Joint Bachelors of Arts in Philosophy and Religious Studies. He also offers personal tuition, analytical marking and consultation to RE and Philosophy teachers.

He is always willing to discuss and share work and resources, and support both students and teachers of the subject. Philosophy is a subject to be shared.

Links, reviews, news and revision materials available on

www.peped.org

www.peped.org website allows students and teachers to explore Philosophy of Religion and Ethics through handouts, film clips, presentations, case studies, extracts, games and academic articles.

Pitched just right, and so much more than a text book, here is a place to engage with critical reflection whatever your level. Marked student essays are also posted.

Published by Active Education

www.peped.org

First published in 2018

ISBN: 9781717906472

Cartoons used with permission © Becky Dyer

All images © their respective owners

Printed in Poland
by Amazon Fulfillment
Poland Sp. z o.o., Wrocław

54106869R00114